MEMOIRS of A LIFE

by J. Patrick Aikman

Plus All-Star
Tidbits, Family
Photos & Poems

Published & distributed by:
J. Patrick Aikman
102 W. Poplar St.
Greencastle, IN 46135

Copyright © 2013 by J. Patrick Aikman.
ALL RIGHTS RESERVED. No part of this book may be reproduced in any manner without the express written consent of the publisher. All inquiries should be made to J. Patrick Aikman at pat.aikman@hotmail.com.

ISBN 978-0-615-84302-5
First Edition

Printed in the United States of America

Front cover photo – Author J. Patrick Aikman, all five-feet-two-inches of him, as a seventh grade member of the Dana School Cobra basketball team (photo provided).
Back cover photos – *Top row (left to right):* The iconic East College bell tower on the DePauw University campus in Greencastle, Indiana (photo provided); a young Aikman displays blue ribbon won in county track meet (photo provided); Aikman family Christmas card "protest" photo from 1969 (photo provided); and a group photo of the boys and girls basketball teams from the 2006 Indiana High School All-Stars (photo courtesy *The Indianapolis Star*). *Bottom row (left to right):* Aikman in first car, a Pontiac, in 1957 (photo provided); Aikman's parents Herb and Charlotte Aikman (photo provided); Aikman with a gathering of friends at a Christmas party (photo provided); and Aikman in Mao cap from a trip to China in 2001 (photo provided).

Cover design by Scott Swain

Cynthia – Always grateful for what you do for Ernie Pyle legend. Best regards.

Pat Aikman
8-10-2015

This book is dedicated to my children John Kevin Aikman, Cindy Sue Robinson, Kerry Gayle Aikman and James Kurtis Aikman, as well as my deceased parents Herbert and Charlotte Jones Aikman and my six grandchildren Emily, Grant, Chloe, Emma, Henry and Michael.

Kaitlin - Blessings
grateful for what
you do for Good Fight
Ragan. God is your.

Pat Gilman
8-19-2016

Acknowledgements

THIS BOOK WAS CONQUERED THROUGH THE exceptional assistance of at least four people: Tina Oetken, a very, generous and very, very helpful librarian at DePauw University's Roy O. West Library, where I spent many hours reading microfilm about the Indiana-Kentucky High School All-Star games from the sports pages of *The Indianapolis Star*; for the informed and technically astute advice and help of a former *Star* colleague Scott Swain who helped steer me through the various aspects of laying out and designing this book, all of which he did with high competence and civility; thanks, too, to David Moeller, half of the Moeller Printing Co. of Indianapolis, who kindly kept me on track and informed about the requirements of book printing; and to my constantly ever-helpful DePauw friend and student, George Velazquez who was always ready to assist me when I was confronted with a computer or printer problem, which it seemed was often. I predict this young Phi Delt Brother will some day likely match Facebook guru Mark Zuckerberg as an entrepreneurial young whiz if he stays on his present track.

A sincere thank you to these kind friends listed above for very dedicated assistance and encouragement.

Contents

Foreword   ix

Chapter One: Memoirs   1

Chapter Two: Photo Memories   81

Chapter Three: All-Star Tidbits   107

Chapter Four: Family Poems   131

Foreword

APOLOGIES ARE EXTENDED IN ADVANCE TO those who may see this book as an attempt at an autobiographical snow job. Initially I wrote this memoir so that my four adult children, Kevin Aikman (Vienna, Austria); Cindy Robinson (Atlanta, Georgia); Dr. Kerry Aikman (Edina, Minnesota); and Kurtis Aikman (Carmel, Indiana), could learn more about their father and what he did during his lifetime to have—if desired—a constant reminder, if consulted, about who their father was and what he did with this time and talent, how he felt about life and his "friends," and what were the issues that concerned him and what was the nature of his work life.

I have included some advice I wish I had received earlier in my life for my children and six grandchildren—Emily Grant, Chloe, Henry, Emma and Michael.

Sports—particularly basketball—has played a huge part in my life; many of my jobs have been sports-connected and many good friendships developed as a result. Most of my grandchildren have participated heavily in sports of one kind or another—from soccer to skiing to baseball and basketball to rowing—and have benefitted in one way or another, learning patience and diligence, sacrifice and disappointment, teamwork and exhilaration and having interesting travel opportunities and travelmates, compassion and sportsmanship—all of which are important to me as part of life's playbook. Did I mention forgiveness? Make a note of it!

I thank all of the kind, generous people who have helped me in my labors at Scottland High School, DePauw University, The Indianapolis Star and in my work with the Indiana Basketball Coaches Association, and the Program of Academic Exchange (PAX) for whom I placed foreign students from Mexico, Brazil, Germany and China with wonderful, caring host American families.

This book is dedicated to my parents, Herbert and Charlotte Jones Aikman, and my four children and six grandchildren—all of whom have made my life and work enjoyable, rewarding, fun and a constant learning and sharing process. Thanks to my old and new friends—near and far.

You, including many coaching friends, all have been important in my life as well as my thoughtful, caring brother Mike of Terre Haute and some of my dear cousins, Lynda Thompson Profitt (Dayton, Ohio); John Harvey Parkay (Battle

Ground, Washington); and Jim Fortune (Clinton, Indiana) and distant cousin, Susan Aikman Miles (Marietta, Georgia) and the three Jenks brothers Jack and Jim and courageous Will "Bill" Jenks, who battled polio from a wheelchair, since we were teenagers on our Dana /Bono farms despite the fact these three "city slickers" lived in suburban Chicago.

I hope you find some pleasure in this fragmented story of my life as much as I did in recollecting it. But I somehow doubt that you will … but thanks for your time and effort, anyway.

James Patrick "Pat" Aikman
Greencastle, Indiana
April 29, 2013

One

Memoirs

JAMES PATRICK AIKMAN WAS BORN ON A SUNDAY, June 2, 1935, on a farm about a half mile north of the Aikman family farm (in the family since the early 1820's) on State Road 71, two and a half miles south of Dana, Indiana, 30 miles north of Terre Haute in Vermillion County. My parents were Herbert Lee Aikman and Charlotte Jones Aikman, deceased in 1999 and 2001 respectively.

Pat attended grades 1 through 12 at the Dana School in Dana, Indiana, enrolling in first grade in 1941, the year the U.S. entered WWII. Pat led an unremarkable life in going through the first eight grades, generally making mostly A's in his studies and reading widely such books as *The Bobsey*

Twins and their activities. He helped his older brother Mike haul water to farm hands who worked in the nearby fields threshing wheat. He and Mike harnessed their ponies to a black buggy and hauled ceramic jugs of water to the workers who were loading sheaves of wheat onto wagons and then hauled it to a huge threshing machine centrally located on various farms including the one owned by Pat's granddad, Burch Aikman and then Pat's father, Herb, who spent his entire life farming the Aikman and Kerns land north of Bono, Indiana. Pat did not enjoy the solitude of the farming life, but preferred the commercial activity of a bustling (at that time) Dana, a substantial farm community of over 1,000 souls during the Second World War, two and a half miles north of the Aikman farm. Pat was not to be a serial tiller of the soil, but his family allowed him to determine his own future.

After Pat's routine birth, he was delivered by his mother's sister, Marzella Jones Parkay Kincaid, a registered nurse who happened to drop by. When a baby, Pat almost starved to death, because 3 year old Brother Mike occasionally snatched his bottle away and drank it). Apparently his parents didn't notice Pat's health decline very quickly. This is an unconfirmed rumor, myth or legend. But he rebounded to a plump 202 pounds by the time he was 65.

Later in the decade the family moved about two miles west of Bono on a gravel road, near an intersection that was just about 100 yards from the C&EI railroad track that connected with the B&O railroad west of Dana with tracks that ran to nearby St. Bernice. Pat remembers very little about living at this site in a modest five room white home, except that he often saw wandering *gypsie*s travel by their home and his mother warned him about being careful around these unknown travelers. He also watched huge, lumbering mechanical tractors rumble by that were used by farmers to power the threshing machines that harvested on a cooperative basis the wheat grown by neighborhood farmers. It was while living here that Pat developed a heart murmur that might have placed him in a Terre Haute hospital for a long stay. (He remembers assembling his clothes in an old black suitcase and taking it with him to see the doctors in Terre Haute one day. Pat has two recollections of these times: (1) observing the fourth of July with a home-developed fireworks show, complete with a couple of bottle rockets in the presence of his folk's very good friends from Metcalf, Illinois, James and Erma Kizer, and (2) Mike and Pat hitching their pony to the tongue of a brand new play wagon and being dragged around the barn lot of the property much too fast and upsetting and destroying the new wagon much to the chagrin of the boys and their parents.

Sometime later, probably in the late 1930s or early 1940, the Aikman's moved to *town,* to the central part of Bono, a crossroads community of probably 12-15 modest homes, peopled by long-time Aikman friends and neighbors—the Bird Malones, the Kernses, Rocky and Fern Martin, Clarence and Mabel Campbell, the Pritchard family including girls Margaret Anne, Agnes May, Rosie and Betty Jean further west of Bono,

Naomi and Sumner Brown, Johnny Aikman and his mother (he was the model on which a *down-home* TV family would later be based) the Spurgeons, the Hathaway boys and their mother and Paul Thomas, a patron and giver of his farm eventually to the family church, the Bono Methodist Church, which Pat and his family for generations faithfully attended and where he learned the early scriptures and observed much of his early spiritual life under the direction of his kind Sunday School teacher Mrs. Bogess & later Sunday School teacher Russell Conner, who taught Pat's class of teenage boys in the church. Meanwhile Pat's parents attended the Merry Sunshine class each Sunday and this young adult class had monthly pitch-in picnics, which were always a highlight of Pat's life that included fun times with the Cheesewright kids (John and Janice), Ronnie Saxton, Max Hendrix, Mart and Kurt Wimsett, and from time to time the Hathaway boys and the Pritchard girls. These parties rotated from home to home and were a feast for those who attended, which included Pat. Mike never enjoyed these picnics,; he would only eat what his mother fixed for the monthly party. Picky, picky, picky!!!!!

Pat enjoyed going next door to the Campbell's country grocery store in Bono, where Mrs. Campbell often had an extra cookie or cracker to share with him. He later would enjoy working in grocery stores as a teenager in Dana at the Grab-It-Here store, and the Harris Foodstore in Clinton as well as at his grandparents' store where he often sprawled on the country store's bare floor in rural Logan, Illinois, about eight miles southwest of Bono, just across the Indiana-Illinois state line. Pat also enjoyed playing in the small creek (AKA as *crick* in Hoosierdom) that ran behind his Bono home, and listened intently to the floor-model radio and its broadcast of the programs that featured "The Lone Ranger," Jack Armstrong, Lum and Abner, and Fibber McGee and Mollie, favorites of most Midwesterners in those pre-TV days. Also Captain Midnight and other sterling serials that captured the excitement of kids' Pats' age and limited culture.

Living in Bono opened up other avenues of adventures, nothing wild mind you, but nature-connected. For example, a small creek ran through the back of the house on property owned not by my family but by someone else. As it turns out Dad and Mom eventually bought the property and its adjoining farm land and the house on top of the hill that ran down to the creek. I spent many a fun day sledding on this hill with Mike in the winter months and other kids and I enjoyed wading in the creek and seining for crawdads, occasionally with my cousin John Harvey, who lived with my Grandpa Silas and Grandma Violet, mom's parents, in the home in Logan, near the Jot 'Em Down grocery store they owned. They owned a nice home about 50 yards west of their store at the east end of Logan, along the main road; the store in addition to the commercial part that stocked the usual staples, included a small attached kitchen and a bedroom near the back of the store but separate that they lived in initially and they occupied when the weather was too bad to walk up the street to their regular domicile. I remember when I was visiting one time that John Harvey and I were playing up the street in a tree near the next door Huffaker house and I fell while jumping from the fence, trying to grab a low tree limb and fell on pieces of jagged concrete that had been left from a dismantled sidewalk. I broke my arm and went to the Paris, Illinois hospital where Auntie Parkay was the head nurse. I was well-taken care of but I remember spending some uncomfortable hours in the bedroom down in the store; it was quiet and rather warm for a 9 or 10-year old. Also from Logan John Harvey and I would occasionally walk over into the Tuttle woods that surrounded a small pond on the farm just east of the store, where JH liked to fish and which we did from time to time. Regular customers at the store were *characters* right out of a book. There was Buffy Underwood who rode his Hawthorne Flyer bike all over, even to Dana, occasionally. Buffy lived alone and was in his 70's or 80's and with a quivering, stubbled chin that always needed a shave, as I recall. He wasn't someone who was a beloved friend, more like a casual acquaintance that everyone knew, but was basically harmless. Buffy lived up the street in Logan near Froggie and Silvia Groves, old family friends of my grandparents and parents. Froggie was a huge fellow and Silvia was a very nice lady who was his wife and who I later encountered as a cook when I taught high school in Scotland, Illinois about 8 or 9 miles north of Logan. JH and I often went mushroom hunting when the season was right, I seldom found many. John Harvey and I were pretty close and I often stayed overnight with my Grandparents and JH and I slept on a rollaway bed on the enclosed back porch of their home. JH was an avid hunter and fisherman and we enjoyed playing with his neighbors Leon Francis and Don Parrish, who lived nearby as well as Dickie Haws, about my brother's age. I recall that one time we had a full blown 'track meet' in the pasture at Dickie's home northwest of Logan. I always lost, it seemed, but I was a successful dashman in 9th grade. There were two particularly key buildings in Logan. One was the long white Town House, next to my grandparents store, just east, and the other was the Logan Public School House, a one-room school house I occasionally visited when I was in 'town.' The Town House was used for township and municipal elections with 'voting booths' in the north end. We often went to the TH to play, for the building it seemed was usually unlocked. It also hosted local celebrations and parties and dances, as I recall. The school house was similar to one in nearby Kidley, where my mother taught in 1931, the mid-1940s and 1950s.

Our next family move was from the home in Bono to the 2-story family, 10-room farmhouse on the family farm, a half mile north of Bono on State Road 71, where I spent the rest of my pre-college days. My grandfather Burch, Dad's father, died in his sleep on a daybed in the family home, where my grandfather and his wife, Gertrude James Aikman, lived for most of their adult life. I think my Dad lived most of his life in this home that was built in 1910 if my memory serves me correctly. I think my Uncle Dewey Kerns, who married my Grandpa Burch's sister, Dolleye, helped build the nice, two-story home that my parents eventually spent a great deal of money on updating it with our first bathroom, electricity, central heating and air, and other improvements such as a lovely enclosed back porch and a comfortable screened in front porch that replaced a traditional wrap-around porch that served as access to the front half of the south side of the house and to the full front of the house. We had a big porch swing on the front porch that was the scene of much of the family entertaining my folks did. I would get on that swing and pump the foot rail to get the swing swaying dangerously fast. I remember my Uncle Leo (Dad's brother) and Aunt Ira from Marietta, GA often wanted to sit on the front porch when they came to visit with their young daughter Susan Aikman Miles, born in 1947. My parents loved to sit by the hours on the newly improved screened-in porch on the southeast side of the house. You could often find them there with my dad sitting in a wicker rocker with his feet perched on the brick ledge that was about 20 inches high that created the brick veneer below the screening on the porches' outer wall. My folks also remodeled the front entrance, rarely used, by creating a small porch with a pitched roof over the front door that led into the large and comfortable living room that they converted from a stark hallway and large, mostly barren room. Mom had this area fully carpeted and fancied up but we used it only occasionally as a teenager, mainly for Christmas parties and other special occasions. She also had book cases built in and a lid that covered the top of the staircase so that the heat from the floor below would not escape into the second floor halfway where I eventually slept as I grew older. My dad repeated a story that we often heard about that he slept in the upstairs hallway when the temperature '*was below zero*.' I slept up there through my high school years and, tucked into the winter blankets, religiously read my bed-side copy of the *Upper Room*, a Methodist publication. This was an oft-repeated tale that Mike and I would introduce when Dad told us of the *hard times* of his youth, which I imagine were actually true, having lived during the Depression as a young married coupe with my mother. They were married May 15, 1930, after eloping and being married secretly in Charleston, Illinois, where my mother was earning her teacher's degree at Eastern Illinois University.

We moved to the family farm after my grandfather's death at age 69 around 1942. My grandmother moved into the upstairs rooms of the family home and had four rooms. I often went up to visit with her and sometimes had meals with her, although she was never was a very good cook, unlike my maternal grandmother in Logan. I remember going into her small store kitchen in Logan and making cookies with her and enjoying her company and love immensely. My grandfather Silas was never a very loving person and often drank excessively, so much so that my grandmother Violet left him from time to time She and her daughters Charlotte and Marzella, often worried about the drinking and carousing he did, but I don't think he ever became violent with Violet, and abusive as so many heavy drinkers do and did. She was a wonderful, endearing grandmother, not much like my grandmother Gertrude, who was loving, but not a very maternal persons as far as I was concerned. But she was always nice to me and I visited her often and admired her ability to write poetry for family events and I think I picked up the desire or knack for doing that from her. She was an intelligent woman and travelled a great deal apparently for those days and our family. My father never liked to travel and didn't, unlike myself. I have traveled over the world (China, England, France, Austria, Switzerland, Chile, Holland, Belgium, Hungary, Israel, Egypt, Canada, Mexico) to learn more about other cultures and geography to my great enjoyment and edification, and for the collection of my foreign hat ensemble. I was always curious about other cultures and enjoyed foreign students. In the past year I placed foreign students with American families: one each from Germany, China, Brazil, and Mexico (Bonnie Ge. Susan Schobert, and Marcos, a lad from Brazil, and Thomas Garma, from Mexico. Here, I am recalling, perhaps with a few unintended gaps, my life and times, in the event you may have discovered this and found it marginally interesting. I wish I were a more capable wordsmith to capture some of the images and thoughts about which I have recently read from the minds of people like author Pat Conroy who wrote about his years at the Citadel and his sometimes rocky relations with his parents and author Laura Hillenbrand and I think often of my passing and wondering if I will have left anything in my life and work that will be of any remark to my children or friends. I do want to live on some way in the minds of those who may have loved me and wish to think about me and my life from time to time. Now,

I am getting maudlin and need to move on to other aspects of my high school and college years and early years of work-life.

What did I do to entertain myself you ask? I was in 4-H, with a variety of projects and I was in the band until high school; I went to movies at the now razed Dana Theatre & played sports. I loved to read but never, for some reason, got into the *classics*. I did like to play the game of croquet. I set up my course on the south side of the front lawn and enjoyed challenging myself as one would on a golf course. Wickets 3 and 5 were at the base of huge, leafy soft maple trees. I once toured my course in 16 mallet strokes … my personal best in those carefree days.

I did not enjoy sitting on a huge tractor all day. I guess one would call me a "people person." I liked to be around people, talking to them about where they lived or used to live, and what they did for a living. I did, however, spend hours at a time on my dad's green and yellow John Deere tractors. My most embarrassing moment was the day I was using a pulverizer behind my tractor to break up clods of soil. I was wheeling down the row apparently happy and oblivious when my brother, Mike, signaled to me from 50 or so yards away that I should turn around and look for my missing equipment, especially the pulverizer, which was about 100 yards behind me in the middle of the 25-acre field. It had come unhitched from my tractor and I was unaware of it. Feeling quite foolish and inept as a would-be farmer, I wheeled my tractor into a tight U-turn and went back for my equipment. Later Mike and I both laughed about it.

When I was about 11 or 12 my mother hired Joan Porter,

a neighbor girl to teach me how to play the piano. Of course, I didn't like it and quit. Now I regret it very much and even bought an electronic piano in hopes I would learn to play, which I have always thought I would do ... but failed to learn or to practice.

My years in the Dana schools were fulfilling and enjoyable in about every way that is discernible. I excelled as a student, based on my grades, made the honor roll while in high school regularly, and graduated as valedictorian of my class. I realize of course, that my competition was minimized, of course, by the size of the high school & lack of classmates; there were only 16 others in my class. Fortunately, at that time we were not required to take SAT tests and with my limited exposure to anything outside the *"culture of Dana and the State of Indiana"* I doubt that I would have done well on these SAT or ACT tests. I guess where I earned my edge in scholastic competition was my enjoyment of studying and reading, including the newspapers, and picking up a great deal of information about the world and fortunately remembering a fair amount of it, at least enough to make people think I was smart or well informed, although that was never an objective of mine—to try to impress people with my knowledge. We had no TV until I was in college. I do remember, however, how much it meant to me when my sixth grade school teacher would often write on the blackboard the total scores each of us earned in the final exams in those years. I could always count on stiff competition from Jayne Ratcliff and John Cook, two people who have remained friends, although living at a distance from me, over the years. I think the one thing, among many I now regret, was that I never thought of the anguish and embarrassment that some of my classmates endured when the teacher would post these test results on the blackboard and some of my classmates would find themselves listed at the bottom of the class standing. I am afraid I thought only of my own outcomes, to the disregard of my classmates. Yet it made me happy to excel and to be noted on the blackboard. My uncle, Charlie Phillips was a custodian at the school and when he erased and cleaned the blackboards, he would often leave our class rankings undisturbed until our sixth grade teacher Mrs. Russell requested a blackboard cleaning to which Uncle Charley obliged.

Unlike many high schools today with numerous special interest clubs, I remember none at Dana, except the Pep Club to which everyone belonged. I was active in 4-H and in successive years my projects included chickens, sheep, a pig and a beef calf which won 10th at the State Fair; my pig, Rosebud, captured Reserve Grand Champion at the Edgar County Fair in Paris, Illinois. I am still very devoted to my 1953 graduating classmates. We have had high School reunions for all alumni, and my class celebrated our 50th, our 55th and are now ready to celebrate the 60th anniversary of our graduation this year (2013) at Turkey Run State Park Inn in conjunction with the Ernie Pyle Fall Festival in Dana. I wish more of my classmates lived in Indiana, but they are living all over the United States.

I did help out on my entrepreneurial brother Mike's Case

baler one summer. The baler scooped up hay or straw into its steel jaws and pushed it into a chamber with a huge plunger. The compressed product came out the rear of the baler in rectangular bales. But first the compressed hay or straw had to be tightly bound with wires. Eddie Bussing, '52, a schoolmate from my school, sat in a metal seat opposite mine and pushed a shuttle into the mass of hay or straw along with baling wire and my job was to tie the ends of the wires together helping to keep the hay and straw compacted and in the form of a bale. One day north of Dana we created over 1,200 bales. To me that was worth a big payday of $18 or 1.5 cents a bale. Mike made considerable money doing custom baling. He has been a farmer all of his 81 years and has much to show for his hard work, diligence and business sense. He also has a condo in Florida which he has generously shared with his nephews and nieces, my children and myself.

    I can't say I didn't enjoy the farm. I did do some light work in the *fruit field* Always excited at Halloween, one year I convinced my dad to let me plant pumpkin seeds in the former—now tillable—pasture that was behind our house. Since my mother told me she liked fried pumpkin blossoms my bumper pumpkin crop served multiple needs. I grew my pumpkins amid the tall cornstalks and also harvested a few blossoms for my mother to prepare.

    As soon as the pumpkins matured, I harvested them and placed them on a rickety picnic table near our driveway and opened the Aikman Pumpkin Market. I did quite well, with prices ranging from 50 cents to a dollar. My first seven or eight years in the Dana grade school (we had all 12 grades in one school building) were unremarkable in most respects other than what I listed above. I recall that I had friends and enjoyed them, but I never felt totally confident that I was sufficiently popular to retain them when the going got sticky or contentious. I did do some noteworthy things in my final years at DHS. Each year the junior class would sell magazines to raise money for our class activities. I was a *super salesman*, selling $329 worth of subscriptions to even another high school at St. Bernice. This figure exceeded all the other classmates and I won a number of minor, unremarkable prizes, including a ukulele. This record for sales existed for more than four years until a girl 4 years behind me, was enabled to top it by assuming the sales of some of her classmates, *or so I was told*, until they exceeded my numbers. I always thought this was unfair but her mother had the reputation for pushing the accomplishments of her own children in a way that turned off some people, including myself. MY parents probably never knew how I felt about this, because by the time it occurred I was long gone to college at DePauw University in Greencastle, Indiana

    I played basketball for four years, earning a starting berth when I became a senior. We won 15 of 22 games and advanced to the quarterfinals of the sectional in Rockville. We lost that overtime game to Montezuma by one point, 31-30, and I will always remember that I shed a few tears that my high school career had ended. However, when I was a sophomore my classmates and I did win the All-School Class tourney, beating the much more talented (presumably) junior class for the championship (I still have a photo of that team with our coach Jack Hendrix in my bookcase. I am kneeling in front with Eddie Scott, who died in 1999 of cancer, shortly after my father died).

In the photo are the author #55, Eddie Scott to my left with a hand on the ball, and our volunteer coach Jack Hendrix, holding our trophy; standing behind us left to right: are David Roe, Dale Hess, Charles Blue, John Cook, Robert "Airplane" Harrington, William "Chick" Potter, and Jimmy "OZ" Marshall. Eddie Scott and Chick Potter are deceased unfortunately.

Another major part of my experience in high school was serving as president of my Junior Class. Why I was singled out for this honor and responsibility I cannot guess, but it was an eye opener for me in several respects. We (the juniors) had the responsibility and duty to operate all the concessions –at the sports events the school hosted as well as noontime when everyone in grade school and high school could come to the Coke Room to buy candy and soda and such, including *Pat's Surprise Packages*. I ruled this operation with a firm hand and came to be known by my classmates as "Big Business!" A name that I initially resented, but eventually came to think of as a compliment. We earned over $1,200 in profits that year and I was always mindful to tell my classmates to always pay for the items they took from the Coke Room and to be sure everyone else did, too. My 'surprise packages' consisted of the remnants of candy bars and such that the mice had chewed into and which I put into small paper bags and labeled them "Surprise Packages." The grade schoolers loved to buy these for 5 cents each. Fortunately, the State and/or Local Health Departments never *nailed* us for such foolish, unhealthy activity. I always "kept the books."

Also during this period I became a paperboy and delivered the now defunct *Indianapolis Times* to homes in Dana, 2.5 miles from our farm. I rode my Wartime (thin tires, wooden-handle bar grips, cheapo) produced bike into town on State Road 71 to pick up and deliver my newspapers. When I was a freshman in high school, I ran track. That is, I competed in the country track meet and won first place in the 50-yard dash and finished fourth in the 100 yard dash. There is a photo of me holding these ribbons somewhere in our widespread archives of Aikman keepsakes. Other honors gained were winning the basketball free throw trophy as a junior for hitting 19 of 29 tosses for a paltry 69%, but that was just enough to win. And I guess that it was the result of setting up a basketball goal in the lot between the house and the barn, where I was a solitary figure practicing my patented underhand two-handed free throw style, seldom, if ever, seen on the gym floors of 2013. In high school, I played under Coach Wally Etcheson, who was a veritable nervous nelly whose style didn't help my weak game or my personal resolve and comfort; Coach Paul Brown, who liked me enough to name his first born son after me*, Patrick* Brown, now about 60 years old, I suspect, and Coach Howard Mathis, an understandably mellow coach who also taught me typing. I played guard, but not very well, just well enough to get on the First Five and to play in every game except the one with Cayuga, when I was at home sick. I scored 140 points that year and had several steals from the opposing team. My best game was a 108-43 blowout of nearby Scottland, Illinois High School during which I scored, for me, what was an unbelievable 20 points. We went to the semi-final game of the sectional that year, losing to Montezuma by one, a team we had beaten earlier in the season by nine. Montezuma went on to win the regional and lost to the Milan Indians, the year (1953) before Milan won the State championship in 1954 behind Bobby Plump and which led to the movie *Hoosiers*.

I also played baseball, second base, and was co-captain of the baseball team. We won the Vermillion County championship on the last day of the season at home in Dana vs. Saint Bernice. I wasn't a very big jock, but like most of the other guys in school, I *participated* and had a lot of fun and camaraderie with the guys. Scott and Roe were probably our best athletes. I believe it was when I was a junior in high school that I got my first car, a 1948 black Pontiac, two-door that had been traded in by our friend Jim Naylor of Dana. Dad negotiated to buy the car and he got it for $1,200. I then drove to school the rest of the year and all the next year. Never had any accidents or fender-benders and my folks were very liberal in letting me use it whenever and wherever I wanted to go, which would not have been an adventure that would have surprised anyone of my age. I had no real wanderlust in those days as a 16-17-18 year old. I think one other kid in my class had a car out of 17 people including nine boys. Many did have access to a family car. Before I got my car I rode the yellow school bus operated by my classmate Jayne Ratcliff's Annie Mae.

In high school I had my first experience acting. I had the male lead or co-lead in two plays, including *Finders Creepers*, that supposedly took place in a funeral home. Pete Hatcher played the role opposite me, a good buddy for real and on the stage. My career as a clarinetist ended, more or less, when I entered high school, after a so-so career on the third row of the clarinet section. I don't remember the name of our play when we were juniors.

My good friend and respected mentor, the Principal John Pickell, notified me some time around the first of May, 1953 that I was going to be valedictorian of my class. That honor earned me throughout my years a good deal of undeserved praise, because everyone I knew at DePauw had graduated with classes even larger than my entire high school (84). I applied for a Rector Scholarship at DePauw but was not interviewed and thus did not get the opportunity to win one. That is something that I greatly regret, but I don't think my folks were aware of the honor and the scholarship support it would have provided. Speaking of DePauw there was never any question of where I would attend college. My mom thought I should go there because my dad's brother, Uncle Leo, attended DePauw and was very successful academically. So classmate Charles Blue and I drove to Greencastle one weekend when we were seniors and spent the weekend living in the Phi Delta Theta house and had double dates with a pair of girls from

Mason Hall, a dorm for independent girls. We had a good time and certainly behaved ourselves. I ultimately pledged the Phi Delt house in the fall Rush period and had many good things happened to me there as a result of the friends/*Brothers in the Bond* I met there and got to know.

Some of my best friends were Jerry "Hare" Jordan, Fritz Knaur, Tom Sargent, Jay Buell and H. Dale Bracey and when I was pledge trainer and Veep, Larry Thomas and Scott Wycoff. But my very best, dependable friend was a classmate from Youngstown, Ohio, Chuck Hinton, who had been valedictorian of his East High School class of 240 students. Chuck died in 1969 of a heart ailment. But back to my valedictory times. Being "V," I got to speak at our high school commencement. My mother was very anxious that I do well, and, of course, so was I. I wrote my speech, "Classmates, Parents, and Teachers and Friends of the Dana School" it began. *"And so, we dedicate our lives to the betterment of the world."* It concluded with, *"For that we were born, for that we were educated, and to that end we pledge our lives."* (I had some coaching from one of mom's lady friends in nearby St. Bernice and memorized the entire one-page speech. I was told I did very well and was complimented by the main commencement speaker who told me I should become a minister, like himself. I should add that some of my favorite teachers were Mrs. Jesse Kerns (history and civics and geometry), Mrs. Chloe James (English) and Mr. Pickell (typing and shorthand). They were no-nonsense instructors and I came to like them very much and always enjoyed their classes in which I was an eager student, *always with my hand up, wanting to be recognized in order to answer the questions they raised. Occasionally, I had the correct answer. In fact, Mrs. James always had a poem on the board, which we were obliged to enter into our little notebooks. One of my favorites was Joyce Kilmer's poem about "Trees." I remember a poem about the two kinds of people, "the people who lift and the people who lean; in which class are you? Are you easing the load of the overtaxed lifter who toils down the road, Or are you a leaner who let's others bear, your portion of worry and trouble and care." Mrs. James also always put a quotation or saying on the board which we were obliged to copy into our trusted little notebook. My favorite was "A grapefruit is a lemon who had a chance and took it." Now that I type it, it doesn't make as much sense to me as it did then. Oh, well. Mrs. James was the grandmother of one of my best grade school friends. Don Eckerty, whose family moved during grade school to Broadlands, Illinois, where I was able one weekend to visit Don and his brother Daryl and their family.*

I guess the highlight of my last year of high school was going to Washington, D.C. for our senior trip. We went by train, my first experience on a train. I loved it, going from Terre Haute to Cincinnati and thence to D.C. We saw all the tourist attractions, the Capitol Building, the Washington Monument (we climbed its 500 feet, naturally), the Bureau of Printing and Engraving, the White House, the Pentagon and viewed the copy of the Constitution. We also went to a low key supper club and enjoyed the dining if nothing else. Mr. and Mrs. Pickell went along as chaperons and we were a pretty calm group. (I think there is a group picture of our class in front of the U.S. Capitol somewhere among my belongings, perhaps in the Black suitcase that is at my son, Kurt's, house in Carmel in storage with many of my other dear collectibles and personal letters.

Immediately after graduation I, without much thought or preparation, took a job as a *salesman* for the Pontiac dealership in Dana, which was located in the two story building directly across the street from the Ernie Pyle museum. I tried to sell cars for Mr. Utley and Mr. Ammerman. I never sold a car and after three days of disillusionment and reality, I quietly left the automobile business though I nearly sold one to classmate John Cook, but we discovered the odometer had been turned back to eliminate mileage. I quietly, without fuss, retired to the farm and helped put up hay, which, if you know anything about "haying" on a farm, you will quickly understand that it is a hot, sticky and difficult job that I quickly decided wasn't for me. I could hardly wait to get off to Greencastle and my second glimpse of college, which was a foreign subject for me, a young, unsophisticated farmer's son from the black, now expensive soil of Helt Township in Vermillion County, Indiana.

My very first memory of my second trip to DePauw was my parents bidding me good-bye along College Avenue just south, down the street away from the then Carnegie Library. It was rather sad at first but I shed no tears. I was astounded when mom later told me that my father cried briefly when he got home, without me, and realized at last that he was facing the 'empty nest syndrome." Dad was never really emotional with me so I was surprised. I don't remember him ever praising me, but maybe he did in his own quiet way; maybe I just forgot, because he was very generous with me; maybe he said at some point during the basketball season, "Good game tonight, Pat." At least my sadness was short lived, for the first person I got to know was Homer Dale Bracey, who would later become my roommate at the Phi Delt house for two years. Dale and I lived together and shared the same double bed when we lived out in town during the one-week rush period, when we both pledged Phi Delt. I still think about that week when I drive by that house on Elm Street, just east of the SAE house, where my son Kevin pledged about 26 years later. Dale was from the "boot heel" of Missouri, Caruthersville, MO. It was to be providential that I pledged Phi Delta Theta because some of the good things, (lasting friendships, a later job at DePauw, membership in organizations, and my interest in journalism) were nourished by that fraternity decision. Garry Boone '54, from Hamilton, Ohio, was president of the house my freshman year and was a mentor to me, encouraging me to get into some activities that interested me. I quickly became a reporter for *The DePauw*, the campus newspaper, and, to my surprise, my 23 pledge class brothers, elected me president of my pledge class, even though they knew little about me or my background or skills or temperament and I was quickly accepted, maybe *quickly* is too sweeping a term, and apparently people in the fraternity saw something about me that somehow, for some reasons, they liked or responded to. Perhaps I had some latent ability that they knew of, but which I didn't then or later recognize. Again, as a junior, I had the happy experience to be elected as the Phi Delt's member on the Inter-Fraternity Council, among 13 campus Greek men. Continuing my work on the campus paper, I was elected Sports Editor, which I greatly enjoyed, and then during the first semester of my senior year I was chosen to be city editor and then editor of *The DePauw* the second semester. It was as editor of the campus paper, *The DePauw*, that I was invited to interview Vice President Richard Nixon in May, 1957 along with the news editor of the campus radio station WGRE. I have the photo of the three of us talking in the Faculty Lounge of the Union Building on my apartment coffee table, next to soon to be President Barack Obama, when he visited my church, St. Luke's United Methodist Church in Indianapolis in 2008. I asked him for his autograph and he carefully wrote it out for me. I have a photo of the two of us. In between these experiences I was chosen to be a member of the Alpha Chapter of Sigma Delta Chi, the honorary journalism fraternity that was founded at DePauw in 1909. This has been an association which has provided many enjoyable experiences and friendships for me over the past 54 years. I owe my selection to SDX to fraternity brothers Mort Berfield, Carmi, Illinois, now an attorney in D.C. and who would not have been a Phi Delt if the members of the house had not ignored the anti-Jewish clause in our national fraternity's constitution and to Dean Berry, deceased, an attorney in Ohio. The two honors I coveted but never received were election to Gold Key, the honorary for senior men who had excelled in leadership on the campus and in academics. I graduated with a 2.65 GPA, on a 4.0 scale, not good enough for GK. The other disappointment I had was not becoming president of the Phi Delt house. I did win election as the house pledge trainer (PT) as a junior: this was frequently the stepping stone to the presidency, and I developed close friendships with several freshmen who I, more or less, tutored as PT, but I failed to win the presidency despite the quiet campaigning of some close friends. And I think it was because I was perceived, not incorrectly by some, who thought I would be a hard-ass in enforcing the no drinking policy in the fraternity. It was not permitted ostensibly in fraternities nor anywhere, even when you were at home, if you were a DePauw student. Since I did not drink, people felt that I would, perhaps, be too rigid in enforcing this regulation.

So I got the runner-up spot as house Vice President, which was an empty honor with little meaningful work to do, I felt. I recall the moral support and care and concern I received through my four years from our wonderful, intuitive housemother Mrs. Grace Gibney, now deceased. I had some great roommates while in the fraternity. There was Homer Dale, with whom I always got along with great (neither of us drank and he became a Presbyterian minister in New York and California so I was in good company always; (he forgave me, I hope, for having two cronies kidnap him from campus and haul him to and dump him on an isolated country road 20 miles from DePauw one night) as part of our traditional ADS vs. SDX Toilet Bowl football game in the fall of our senior year. Part of the tradition was kidnapping each teams' players. I was kidnapped from a downtown barbershop and tied up in the Phi Gam house, but escaped before "execution." I don't even remember who won the game the next day; Bob Burney, whose father was Surgeon General of the U.S.A., and my close friend Chuck Hinton, from Youngstown, Ohio, where he was raised in a family of four boys in a blue collar family in this important Steel Town in which his father was engaged. I remember my first really lengthy trip in my car was a 400-mile sojourn to Youngstown during the summer of 1954, when I drove to see Chuck and his family and spent four or five days with them. Chuck had been valedictorian of his class of 240 at East High School in Youngstown and was a Rector Scholar until his grades slipped beneath the level which you had to maintain to retain your scholarship. That ultimately led to Chuck's having to leave DePauw during the summer of 1955 when we both decided to stay in the Phi Delt house and work at the newly opened IBM plant in Greencastle during the day and at the Union Building at night. We both ran machines that printed the punch cards that were used in early computers.

One of the saddest days in my college years occurred one day when I came home from work at IBM and found a note on my desk that Chuck had written when his Dad, who had come to pick him up and take him back to Youngstown, insisting that they leave Greencastle immediately without saying goodbye to me, ending our summer in the frat house. It was a difficult thing for me to accept that his dad had been so unkind to the feelings of both of us, but I suspected that he was not particularly a sensitive man, but literally a man of Steel. Chuck was not to return to DePauw until after I graduated in 1957. He did ultimately return though, and received his degree from the university. Shortly after Chuck left, I moved from the fraternity to an upstairs bedroom in the home of our main cook at the Phi Delt house, Mrs. Kimball, who lived one block from my frat house on Anderson Street. I lived there the rest of the summer until school resumed in the fall. One of my best friends after Chuck left was classmate and frat brother Fritz Knaur, who lived in Greencastle and was a 'townie" attending DePauw. Fritz died a few years ago in Michigan, where he was a psychologist.

I guess I became a serial resident of Greencastle, living here the summer of 1956 and, indeed, 1957, working on *The Greencastle Daily Banner,* as a reporter at large and at the Union Building, where I closed up the building and the cash register in the Hub and deposited the money in a bag at the Central National Bank. The summer of 1956 I lived with a widowed lady out on the east side of town, near the President's home in a small, home and the next summer I lived in a two-story home across the street from the Phi Delt house in an apartment that was rented by our house adviser, Dr. Hans Grueninger, head of the German department. Dr. G. let me live in the apartment without rent. He was a very kind man who was still teaching at DePauw when I returned to work there in 1960. My academic work as a student was not sterling, as my GPA above points out. It wasn't that I didn't study, but I had so many other interesting things to do ... like the newspaper and the organizations I was involved with and fraternity affairs. I majored in American History and my adviser was Dr. Andy Crandall, an expert on the Civil War. I enjoyed his classes as well as my classes in Spanish, which I took for 19 hours, just short of a minor. I actually also took a Spanish Drama class, thinking I could cut it, but I did not take easily to the language and wound up earning a C in the course, I did have a B 3.0 average a semester or two during my four years. I do recall getting a D in a mid-semester examination in psychology and this is the grade that was reported to my parents when mid-semester grades were sent out. Believe me, I received considerable communications after the mail was delivered to Dana, I ultimately received a C in the three hour course. That was the only time that my parents expressed to me any dismay about my study habits and grades.

One of the most unpleasant experiences I had when I was editor of *The DePauw* came as a result of missing a final exam in my one education course, which I took in order to gain my teacher's license. In one of my paper's editions, I had printed a column by two Phi Psis that criticized the education requirements for teaching licenses. The teacher who I had for my education course cut the article out and gave me as my make up exam (my maternal grandfather Jones had died in January 1957 and I had attended his funeral). It was a test that quoted the article from the paper and instructed me to point out the errors in the column as facts go and was generally unfair in what it expected from me as far as a typical final examination. I took the egregious exam questions out to my newspaper advisor, Dr. Fred Bergman and told him what had happened. He said, "That son of a bitch." I subsequently wrote an editorial in the newspaper denouncing in the third person this kind of personal attack on a student, without naming the professor who gave the test or identifying myself as the student. The end result of this was that I received a C in the course. The irony of this event was that about 20 years later the professor of education who inflicted this bizarre exam, (Dr. Herb Heller) on me befriended son Kevin, and hired him to work on the pipe organ at the Presbyterian Church in Greencastle. Kevin enthusiastically did the work in a timely fashion and walked away with a check for $900 from the work for which he was tremendously underpaid, since he was a high school senior and not a professional organ repairman in the strictest sense. But he would have probably done it for less for he was deeply interested in this kind of work and excelled at it. I recall that we had organ parts strewn for weeks over much of the large playroom of our home at 801 Highwood Avenue.

One of the more memorable experiences I had during the last couple years of my high school enrollment and for the first couple of college years was working at the Indiana State Fair. I was there for the 100th anniversary, working in what was then called the Women's Building. About 10 guys my age lived and cooked and bathed in a couple of rooms off the second floor exhibition space. Two of my friends from Dana, Denny Barker and Charles Blue both worked with me. We were responsible for assisting the adult women with checking in the entries of Hoosiers who entered canned goods, cakes and pies and other goodies for the competition that could have earned them money, prestige and beautiful ribbons. We were responsible for cleaning and polishing the windows of the multiple display cases, sweeping out the trash that accumulated on the floors of our area, The Culinary Department, and policing the viewing area where people came and sat on the ledges of the overlook to watch the L.S. Ayres style shows that were a prominent feature each year of the Women's Building. When we had completed our work each day we were free to attend events at the fair or visit the various other displays, events and rides that made up the fair. We cooked our own meals and did our own shopping to minimize our expenses while we were in Indianapolis for the three-week experience. We were paid what seemed to me at the time a princely sum of over $60 per week … a nice little payoff to start the new school year. I think my DePauw tuition my last year was $700, but I had to take 18 hours to get my education courses at an extra cost of $450 but my parents wanted me to graduate and paid the extra charge. Now tuition is close to $40,000 plus room and board.

    One memorable trip I made as a student was when I was a sophomore taking ROTC. The Air Force was attempting to draw additional students into Advanced ROTC and a group of us ROTC students were flown in a C-47 to San Antonio, Texas, for an introductory tour and visit to Lackland Air Force Base.

That was my first airplane flight and I did enjoy it even though we had to sit on our butts in the frugal, stripped down interior of the troop plane. I was 19 or 20.

If it seems that most of my concentration has been on extracurricular affairs and goings on during my four years at DePauw, that's probably not an incorrect surmise. I enjoyed doing things and being involved with my classmates. Some of my best friends at that time were fellow newspaper workers—Jo Petry, a fellow editor from Hoopeston, Illinois, whom I still stay in touch with now that she is Mrs. Dick Hershberger of Wakarusa, Indiana; Joanie Moore Mernitz, Indianapolis; Dick Hackenberg, Chicago advertising executive.

Now as well as several other guys who were buddies then, plus Reed Scism, who later became a lawyer in Indianapolis and whose grandson is on my grandson Michael's baseball team in Carmel, Indiana and Dr. Al Millett, Columbus, Ohio. In addition to my studies and activities I also worked as a waiter at the Phi Delt house and as a sports information assistant to the director of the DePauw University News Bureau. I kept sports stats for Don Tourtelot at football and basketball games at home and on the road. As a matter of fact when I returned to work at DePauw I took the job which Don T., in an angry state of mind, had resigned from and was somewhat familiar with the nature of his work, particularly the sports work that he and I did.

Our class of 1957 graduation was June 10, 1957 on the Blackstock Stadium turf. I'll never forget marching out to the stadium in our somber black robes to hear the commencement keynoter Thomas Watson, president of IBM Co. The one thing I have regretted over the years is that I did not demonstrate or express to my parents how much I appreciated and the fact that they, though their financial help and moral support, enabled me to gain a degree (I did graduate in the upper half of my class as it turned out but that was no big deal other than a mathematical happenstance) and considerable experience and friendships while at DePauw. I remember sitting in my new green and white 1957 Buick in front of the Alpha Phi house, talking to Judy before we both departed campus that day when all of her family including her grandmother came. She was a Hoosier and loved the fact that Judy's boyfriend was also a Hoosier. "Queenie" Folk had lived in Flora, or Camden, Indiana, before moving to Chicago where her husband ran and owned a coal company.

As I recall both Judy and I pledged to see each other over the summer, and that we did. She came by train to Dana via Clinton many times and her parents came as well to meet my parents in our Dana home. And I made several trips on weekends to Oak Lawn to visit her and her parents. One amazing episode that summer unfolded when I was taking Judy to catch the train back to Oak Lawn in Clinton. Just north of Clinton a passenger train crossed the road ahead of us. I said, "Judy there goes your train and you've missed it." We spun around and raced the train to Danville, Illinois, watching across the verdant fields as the train raced out of our sight. When we finally pulled into the station at Danville, shortly after the arrival of "our" train I told

Judy to get her ticket and I would wait at the steps of the train with the conductor. I breathlessly said to him," The train to Chicago/Oak Lawn is a bit early today, isn't it?" He said, "Oh no, that train won't be along for a while yet." Judy and I both could laugh now about our ridiculous and probably unsafe needlessly mad dash from near Clinton some 30-40 miles north to Danville, Illinois.

This was a memorable summer for me—1957. While Judy and I saw each other pretty regularly on weekends, I finally proposed to her during one of the weekend visits. She accepted, although she told me, as I recall, that she was going to graduate school in California if I had not proposed. We set the date of our marriage as November 30, 1957, in Oak Lawn, Illinois. I continued to pursue my teaching job through the fall semester and following Thanksgiving that year, made my way to Oak Lawn for the wedding. I went up a few days early and not knowing, which was ridiculous, the proper etiquette for weddings, attended the rehearsal dinner, given by the Reiners in their home. (The groom's parents normally are expected to provide the rehearsal dinner, I was later to learn, though Judy never said a word about this social faux pas nor did her parents.) I was embarrassed and wondered why Judy never mentioned it to me then or later. Anyway, my parents came from Dana, which somewhat surprised me that my Dad would venture to drive 150 miles from home, which he was not apt to do at any other time in his life as far as I knew). My groomsmen included my cousin John Harvey Parkay, my brother Mike, and my best college friend Chuck Hinton from Youngstown. Judy's bridesmaid included Mike's wife, Jeanne as I recall but am uncertain, Judy Buckner Rose, and another sorority sister, plus Judy's dear rather unconventional sister Jean who later died of cancer in 2000, leaving a son, Darian. The minister was the man who was presiding minister of the Congregational Church, Judy's church in Oak Lawn. A reception dinner was held in the church basement following the wedding. Judy and I returned to Dana after the wedding to occupy our new home, in the apartment on the second floor of the Ammerman's home on Dana's Main Street. Two days later I returned to teaching and coaching at Scotland High School, foregoing the honeymoon that we never had and which we eventually took, although we never called it that, on a trip to (Europe; Holland, France, England, Italy Austria, Switzerland) via Pan Am in April-May, 1987 while I was on sabbatical from DePauw. I also spent time visiting the PR staffs of Southern Methodist University in Dallas and at Clemson University in Clemson, South Carolina.

After graduation, I sought and was hired as a school teacher at Scotland, Illinois High School, about 10 miles west of Dana, and where I knew at that time several people, including adults, who had know and liked my grandparents, visiting and trading at their little grocery in Logan, Illinois.

I was hired to teach English and coach the grade school basketball teams. I loved teaching and directing the Senior class play and all the other usual activities that one encounters when in the teaching profession. I also, eventually, taught Spanish, history, English and civics and was advisor to the school paper. I had a supportive principal, Mr. Henry Grice, and later a gentleman by the name of Mr. Rossi. My second year at Scottland, Judy decided to teach there, despite saying in the years before that 'she'd rather dig ditches than teach school." I think she enjoyed her teaching and did a good job at it; The students liked her and I think they liked me. The second year of my work at SHS found me getting the virtual ultimatum that if I was going to teach in high school, I needed to coach the high school boys basketball team, moving up from grade school coaching. I guess, after having won the county tournament with the grade school boys the year before, the school board thought I was some kind of John Wooden. I must admit that I went into the job, not knowing much about the fundamentals of basketball. (The reasons I was faced with this *fait accompli* was that the high school coach resigned from his teaching position shortly before the basketball season began and I was a marked man, destined to be willing conspirator in the game of basketball. We did have a few boys who were as good or better than I was in high school, not saying much for my skills. They were a nice group of boys and were willing to do what their rookie coach asked them to do. And that was *WIN*! That year, if I remember correctly, we won seven games and lost 15, which for Scottland, was a fruitful season. Our best players were Mike Eslinger, later sheriff of Parke County; John Hixon, Kenny Grubb, Richard Fulton, Ronnie Bolen and Maurice Straw. I just remember that as coach of the grade school team, I arranged a trip for the boys to Oak Lawn, Illinois, where Grandpa Folk, Judy's dad, arranged for us to play one of the Oak Lawn grade school teams, an extended trip unlike any my boys had ever participated in going to Chicago, and, of course, we drove through downtown Chicago and past the White Sox Stadium … a first for virtually all of these home grown kids. We did win the game. Also in another effort to give my teams a unique—for the high school team—basketball/travel experience—we played a team, Breese, Illinois, just across the Mississippi River from St. Louis. We stayed in a hotel in St. Louis and also dropped by the St. Louis airport—for me this was probably something I liked and thought my team would also enjoy. Why? I don't know. Anyway in the St. Louis Airport, we encountered a candidate presumably running for the presidency of the U.S. and his name was Stuart Symington. This was probably in 1959 and I think the man was from Missouri. Anyway, we lost the two games to Breese, but I still think the experience of the kids making this trip was something that they otherwise would never have been able to participate in … and I was happy about that … giving them an experience they otherwise would never have had. One of my fellow teachers at Scottland was a fellow named Harvey Brewington, who had married Betty Hixson of Dana, and they lived in Dana and often Harvey and I would trade driving responsibilities. I should also mention that for one year when I was at Scottland, my brother's first wife, Jeanne Russell Aikman, taught at the school as well. She taught home economics. She was a bright, attractive, very personable woman who had been Mike's classmate at Dana High School in the class of 1950.

In the spring of 1960 I received a call from my Phi Delt brother Gary Boone. He told me that the director of the DePauw News Bureau had resigned and encouraged me, if I were interested, to get in touch with DePauw, which I did. I drove to DePauw during the tail end of the Scottland Eagles' basketball season and interviewed with Dr. Russell Humbert, president of DePauw and with Norman Knights, director of development who would become my boss. I think my interviews went sufficiently well and I was invited to join the administration at the university. Driving home from the interview, I was given a speeding ticket north of Greencastle and the trip cost me about $20, not including gas which was about 39.9 cents a gallon.. Not a very important item to include here, but just something that registered on my brain stem as I write this. After arriving home that night, we had to play Brocton in the high school tourney in Chrisman, Illinois. We lost the game by 4 points and played well … and with both regret and impending excitement, I submitted my resignation at Scottland shortly thereafter. But the last item on my Scottland agenda was, with my wife, Judy, chaperoning the senior class on its train trip to Washington, a repeat vacation of my own experience while a senior at Dana High School. Judy was pregnant with Kevin when we took this trip to the nation's capital.

I failed to mention that after our wedding, we chose an apartment on Dana's Main/Maple Street, owned by the

Ammerman's to settle in. It had a kitchen, one bedroom and a living room and a large bath. We had bought some Danish furniture at a store in Beverly, near Oak Lawn, that comprised our furnishings in the living room. My mom and dad gave us a kitchen dining set for our wedding present. I don't recall where we got the bed, perhaps from the Ammermans. This house had stately white wood columns in front and it is still on the site today although it is in somewhat of a distressed state. I visited there in 2012 to purchase some candy from an entrepreneur who recently opened this shop on North Main Street, much to my delight for Dana.

After our first year in the Ammerman apartment we decided to move into a larger, more spacious abode, and drove to Paxton, Illinois to see if my dad's cousins, Kathleen and John Swinney, who owned the home formerly occupied by my grandfather Burch's sister, Dolleye Aikman Kerns (known to me as Auntie Doll), would rent Judy and me the house, which they seemingly with joy did for the reasonable price of $40 per month. Judy and I quickly drove to Terre Haute to Wiebolt's Furniture Store, and purchased some expensive furniture which we kept throughout our married life and which Judy as of 2013 still maintains. It included a lovely table and six chairs and an all-wood buffet in which we kept our silverware and our extra dishes. We also purchased some large sections of carpet and other odds and ends to spruce up our commodious home. Our new home in Dana included a vast wraparound porch in front and along the east side, plus a large living room and fireplace, plus a large dining room and an adjoining library/family room, which we converted into a downstairs bedroom, and a medium sized kitchen. We also had an enclosed back porch and a two car garage, which was more than enough for our, by then, new 1959 Buick. We also had a nice little porch outside our kitchen on the east side of the house.

It was also nice to have a large, unimproved lot west of the house on which we planted flowers in one corner. It still in 2013 is unimproved, apparently waiting for a landscaper or vegetable gardener to utilize all the space. Queenie Folk, Judy's grandmother, had given us a lovely desk for our wedding which we used regularly in the living room along with the two Danish sofas. This is the home to which Kevin was born on a hot, steamy day on July 7, 1959. We drove to the Clinton Hospital that morning about 8 a.m. Judy was in labor for about eight hours and Kevin was born about 4 p.m. I had never seen a newborn baby and was shocked at the wrinkled face little guy that the nurse presented to me in the lobby outside the nursery. Kevin would have, eventually, a difficult time sleeping and eating when we returned to our home. He cried, it seemed, every night for some time and had a skin problem, which required considerable attention. But he was a healthy baby and I learned so much about being a parent that summer. I can remember sitting on the front porch of our rented Dana home, swinging in the large front porch swing singing "Little John Kevin, Little John Kevin, time to go to sleep, time to go to sleep." I don't think he was listening.

At this point I pick up the thread again of our move to Greencastle in the spring of 1960. On about June 20 we moved from Dana to Greencastle to begin my work at DePauw as the director of the News Bureau and Sports Information. I remember Dad moved us in his big red truck with the stock racks on it. Max Smith, his hired hand, Dad and Mike pitched in.

We found a delightful little Cape Cod type home at 7 Park Street, about one block from the campus, near the Kappa Alpha Theta house and Longden Hall, where Uncle Leo had lived some 30 years previously. Our new home had two stories, two upstairs bedrooms, with a small kitchen, small family room, dining room and comfortable living room, plus a full bath and a half bath upstairs and downstairs, respectively. It had a one-car garage and a usable back yard, which we fenced it, now that Kevin was one year old, and Cindy was born about one month after we moved to Greencastle on July 8, 1960.

Judy returned to the Clinton Hospital to deliver Cindy who was born exactly 366 days after Kevin's birth in the same hospital. I remember that my grandmother Gertrude Aikman was in the hospital at the time Cindy was born. The day after her arrival, I received a call from the hospital that she needed a blood transfusion, I hurried to the hospital and they had taken blood from her mother and transfused it into Cindy and she came through with beautiful flying colors. Fortunately, Cindy did not have the insistent colic that Kevin experienced, so her birth was not as traumatic as Kevin's post birth was. She slept and thrived without the complications that accompanied

Kevin's entry into the world. After her birth, we returned to Greencastle to deal with two tiny, lovable babies in our rapidly expanding home life. I renewed my training in changing diapers.

    I began my work at DePauw that summer, working out of my office in the basement of Studebaker Administration Building. I was fortunate to inherit the secretarial services of Mrs. Jake (Mary) Hirt who remained with me almost to the end of my enjoyable years at DePauw. I think she retired sometime in the late 1970's or early 1980's. I enjoyed my work, writing stories about events and activities at DePauw which I thought were newsworthy to the press in Greencastle as well as elsewhere beyond our borders. This might be news about an important campus speaker, a faculty development, a concert or a particularly important sports event. Since there were many athletic encounters both in Greencastle and on other campuses, I frequently 'went on the road' with the team, especially in basketball, which I enjoyed greatly. I think my first big road trip with the basketball team was to New York City where the Tigers were to play Fordham, and Army. A scheduled stop on this trip to NY City included a visit with DePauw alum Barney Kilgore, editor of *The Wall Street Journal*, in his offices. The games at Fordham and Army were losses, but little did I realize that one of the Army coaches was the rambunctious Bobby Knight. There were no explosions or chair-throwing in this encounter as DePauw went down rather easily. But it was eye opening to see historic West Point and where all the cadets, including at one time Benedict Arnold, the famous traitor in Revolutionary War lore, lived and studied. I also drove to most of the DePauw football games all of which, with perhaps some few exceptions, were played in Indiana. I frequently took along on these trips my friend, art professor Dick Peeler, who was in the art department and who filmed the games for later use by Coach Tommy Mont. Frequently Kevin, Cindy and Kerry went along as well for the excitement. I enjoyed having my children with me. They were very verbal and interested in the day's activities.

Where do I begin to start with a description of my career/life at DePauw? Judy, Kevin and I moved by Dad's truck to Greencastle in mid-June 1960. Our neighbors across the Street were Kenny and Chloe Bennett: Kenny was the owner and publisher of one of Greencastle's two newspapers. Chloe was a wonderful, caring, interesting neighbor and she had two sons and one daughter, Suzy who married my fraternity brother Fritz Knaur, now deceased in Michigan.

My new job was called Director of the News Bureau at DePauw, and I succeeded Don Tourtelot, for whom I worked in sports while I was at DePauw. I was hired by President Humbert, a former Methodist Minister, and I reported to a man who became a long-time friend Norman Knights, director of development at DePauw. In all the years I worked at DePauw under Mr. Knights, we never had a disagreement or confrontation. He was always very supportive and more or less let me do my job without interference or *hovering*.

My job was to ferret out stories that would be appropriate and newsworthy to the local and wider media. This was something that I was comfortable doing, because I had done much of this as editor of *The DePauw*. I remember my first story was about a conference/convention that the Alpha Chi Omegas were to hold on the DePauw campus. My office was in the basement of the Studebaker Memorial Administration Building on South Locust Street, where it still stands. I felt reasonably at ease doing this job as well as handling reporting of DePauw's athletic teams and the results of their competition with other colleges. I kept statistics for football and basketball and reported these by phone to *The Indianapolis Star* and the wire services, AP and UPI, well before the introduction of the computer and internet. Another thread in my job description was to serve as liaison with the media when they wanted information about DePauw or about things that were happening here. This became a major source of my concern and professional behavior during the Student Protest years, surrounding the Vietnam War and other student acts of disobedience or protest ... we never had any acts of violence except the burning of the AFROTC building by a couple of students!

I was called to the office of President Kerstetter, who had succeeded President Humbert, following his sudden and untimely death during 1962. The meeting with President Kerstetter was to discuss the fallout of the burning of the ROTC building. It seemed that two students, or perhaps it was one, had turned up at Putnam County Hospital with severe burns on his body. The young man's name was Clark Adams from Delphi,

Indiana. Clark had been on the freshman basketball team and I had come to know him and liked him very much. Clark was not a bad kid at all, but was inclined to go off the deep end sometimes. He was, after this episode, in the deep end!

He was hospitalized in Indianapolis for many months with his injuries/burns, and I went up to see him one time. We had a good visit and I don't think he was ever punished in the usual sense of serving time in prison or jail, but was ordered by the local Judge Hamilton not to return to Putnam County for a period of years.

This incident was a major development for me to handle and I think I handled it sufficiently well. President Kerstetter, as I have previously stated followed Pres. Humbert in the president's office. I recall that I met with Academic Dean Robert Farber at his home to learn the news that President Kerstetter would be coming to DePauw from Iowa's Simpson College. I attended the Board of Trustees meeting in Indianapolis at which he was introduced and briefly spoke. I don't recall the exact details, but he turned out to be a *unique* person to work with. When I had a story to write that concerned him or something of importance to the University, especially a gift of substance, I would generally submit it to him for his perusal because he always wanted to see and know how it was being presented to the media.. It always came back with a bunch of scribbles all over the page, written upside down and in all the margins. I kept a number of the original copies of these stories and bequeathed them to the DePauw Archives, for I thought they would reflect the type of person that Dr. Kerstter was. He was concerned about any nuance that would reflect poorly on him or the university. Of course, *I was alert* to the same thing and obviously never wrote anything in that context or of that nature. But one could never predict what would trigger his penchant for changing a phrase or omitting it all together. I learned to be very careful in how I wrote for his whims.

Dr. Kerstetter was, it seemed, never really comfortable with many people. And he was not inclined to joke or kid around … but was always overly serious and definitely not charismatic. I had two or three occasions when I felt I had incurred his wrath or displeasure. He never lashed out at me at anytime, but it was apparent when he was unhappy about something. I believe that his wife, frequently conveyed for him, his displeasure of things that bothered him, although I never had an unpleasant experience with her. She was not an easy person to "read."

I do recall one Christmas time that four of us who worked with Dr. Kerstetter were invited to the President's home for a small social gathering that included the Sanders, the Cooks and I think Glenn and Betty Job. I wondered why we were invited to such a small, elite party … perhaps the Kerstetters were *reaching out* to a group with whom they felt comfortable. I never could figure it out; however, I do remember that I took a gift and it was a painting of Dr. Kerstetter that had been done by Sports Illustrated when they came to campus to do a story about the Monon Bell football game. I had been given this drawing by SI for some reason, I can't recall. Anyway, after I had done this, I regretted I had given this away and not kept it for myself or for the Archives. I do recall that I got to know the SI reporter who did the story, John Feinstein, the author of the Bob Knight expose *Season on the Brink* and I was quoted in SI for some meaningless remark in the story. I don't think Dr. K felt particularly honored to receive the drawing, but to me it was of note.

I'll never forget what would be an embarrassing event connected that year with The Monon Bell game. *THE GAME* between DePauw and Wabash for one-year possession of the Monon Bell, the 350-pound bell taken from atop a locomotive operated at one-time by the Monon Railroad which runs through Greencastle and Crawfordsville and for which the two colleges have battled each year for 80 consecutive years since 1932. The entire history goes back to about 1894 and over 100 games. We like to say it is the "oldest continuous football rivalry west of the Alleghenies." Now back to the theft of The Bell.

A number (perhaps 2 or 4) of Wabash students came to see Dr. Kerstetter, introducing themselves as from Mexico in some good neighbor capacity. They told him they had heard about the "famous Monon Bell game" and asked if by any chance they could look at the bell. He apparently thought it was a legitimate request and fell for the ruse. He instructed Dr. Jim Loveless, the then Athletic Director, to show them the Bell which was stored in a building out near Blackstock Stadium. Late that night the Bell was stolen by Wabash students. It was definitely an embarrassment to Dr. Kerstetter, but he never mentioned it to me or to anyone else as far as I know, but the media in the area made a great deal of the successful masquerade and the heist of the Bell was the life of the News Bureau Director in those halycon days.

Somewhere, amid all these monolithic events, was the birth of our third child and second daughter, Kerry Gayle Aikman, in the Putnam County Hospital, around 10 p.m. on Sept. 27, 1961. Judy and I had obtained from somewhere a beautiful antique crib in which we placed little Kerry when we brought her home. I do recall one night when I went to visit Judy and Kerry in the hospital that her roommate observed to her when she saw me, "I see that you married an older man." I never did learn what Judy's response was but we brought Kerry home to Park Street and she whiled away her time in the lovely crib. Kerry was a good baby who didn't cry a lot, as Kevin did when he was born and carried on continuously in his first year. I recall that her arrival preceded by about four days my reporting for active duty to the U.S. Air Force Reserve unit at Terre Haute's Hulman Field. Our National Guard F-84 fighter squadron there was activated, along with several military units in the USA.

During the Cuban Missile Crises, the U.S. blockaded Russian ships that were attempting to deliver missiles to a port in Cuba. When met by U.S. Naval Forces, the Russian ships reversed their engines and returned to the Soviet Union. This was claimed by the Kennedy Administration as a great Cold War success, and I guess it was.

Nevertheless, my squadron had been activated and I spent the next 11 months commuting from Greencastle to Hulman

Field in Terre Haute to complete my active duty commitment. We were finally released from active duty in August of 1962. I was an Airman First Class non-commissioned officer and my duties while in the service were in information services, essentially like the work I was already doing at DePauw. However, I did produce and edit the base newspaper while at Hulman Field and did go on a two-week joint maneuver with the Army at Eglin Air Force Base near Pensacola, Florida.

It was about this time that Judy and I decided we wanted to build our own home. We had visited several model homes in the Chapel Hill sub-division on the west side of Indianapolis and found a builder we liked. His name was Bob Bruce of Bruce-Zieger Construction. We immediately liked Bob and even more-so when we learned that he had graduated from DePauw. I had made some preliminary drawings of a house that we thought would fit our needs and gave the drawing to Bob. He then developed a professional blueprint and construction started in September, 1962. We built it on a lot we bought from DePauw and got a mortgage through DePauw for about $17,500. The house cost us $17-18,000; it was finally paid off in 1988, the same year I started a new job with *The Indianapolis Star*. The house contained four bedrooms, one for each of our (then) three kids and a master bedroom, plus a bath upstairs and a half bath downstairs; we had a family room in which we had the TV and the kids' rocking chairs thanks to Judy's parents, plus a living room with a dining room table at the north end and a very small galley kitchen which was very tight for all the cooking Judy had to do, plus a two-car garage. Rather crowded, but we loved it until we put on a 1100 sq. ft. addition for $12,500 in 1969. We added a long family/play room, a formal dining room, and a nice large master bedroom downstairs with a full nice bath and tub. Our first Christmas in the house, we had a photo taken by my good friend and neighbor Ralph Taylor with the kids on the stairs with Judy and me and sent this card to all of our friends. This became a Christmas tradition in our family for several years and people got to expecting these family cards each year in December. We continued this until about 1979 or so and each year I would go up to Ralph's studio on Washington Street and printed the 100 or so cards that we would send out each December. People got so they began collecting the cards and son Kurt actually had all of the cards over the years framed, and last I checked he had all the framed cards in his home in Carmel. Usually some kind of poem or *clever* prose accompanied or projected the Christmas message.

But back to DePauw. The late 60's and early 70's were a tenuous time in fraternities for those who would advise them, as I did the Phi Delts. I remember we had a boy in the house from Yellow Springs, Ohio, who we found was apparently selling drugs out of the Phi Delt house and creating a real liability problem to say nothing about the appropriateness of his actions for the Phi Delts. The members of the House Corporation and I met and discussed this issue and decided that we had to dismiss the young man from the fraternity. We all speculated as to what the reaction of the rest of the boys in the house would be. It turned out that they did not argue the decision. We also had the problem of so many large dogs in the house. Many boys wanted to have their own family dog live and romp–and poop– in the house. This was hard on the furniture and carpets and was an issue we had to deal with. Six dogs were dismissed and sent home. I think it was an issue that the house officers did not want to deal with. So the House Corp. did!

In 1974, after seven years as house advisor and member of the House Corp., I resigned from both positions. I recall that the then House President remarked to me, "It shouldn't be too hard to replace you." That pissed me off, but I didn't say anything. The least I could have expected was a sincere thank you, but so many kids just don't have that perspective or appreciation for certain things that are done on their behalf.

Earlier in the decade of the 60's I assisted, in a small way, in helping Garrett "Gary" Boone, the new house advisor and HC officer is realizing the building of the new addition on the back of the house. The curved cement roofed addition was designed by Evans Woolen of Indianapolis who designed the Main auditorium at Butler's Clowes Hall; Garry was very impressed with Mr. Woolen and greatly admired his work. In addition to my media duties at DePauw I was also active in the professional organization that included media, PR and development/advancement people. It was called the American College Public Relations Association or ACPRA. With our family, we attended many of the ACPRA national conventions around the USA.

Judy and I drove to Denver for a conference one summer, the summer in which Kevin was born, 1959; We also took a family trip to Miami, FL one summer for the ACPRA conference and stopped in some Florida town to visit Grandma Folk's sister and her husband en route to Miami' We stayed in the Fountainbleu Hotel there. Another time we drove to Boston for the summer conference and I remember Judy took the kids to see the home of Paul Revere and did other sight-seeing in the city. We also drove to New York City for a conference and the kids got to see the sights of that bustling city.

I was fairly active in ACPRA and was asked in 1971 or 72 to plan the conference that was held in Chicago that year. I spent a lot of hours and made many calls to do this chore and found it very rewarding, being asked if I would permit myself to be nominated to the Board of the regional ACPRA. For some silly reason, I declined this opportunity, which leads me to talk a moment about a response or personal quirk that I never understood about myself.

A number of what I considered nice opportunities have come to me, unexpectedly and unsolicited, and I have accepted the challenge. What always found its way into my mind was how could people I barely knew give me these opportunities/honors. For example, when I was elected president of my class as a high school Junior, when I was elected president of my 24-member Phi Delt pledge class as a freshman, when I hardly knew anyone very well in the house after a few weeks. And when I later was elected Pledge Trainer and Vice President of the House as a sophomore and junior, respectively, and then house representative to the Interfraternity Council (KTK). Did I fail to live up to the expectations of others or did I fail to capitalize on all the opportunities I had come my way for one reason or another.

As I have thought about this issue I have begun to feel that I could have done something really important or meaningful in my life that, if I had only had a plan or certain ambitions or goals and knew what they were and how to attack and fulfill them, that I would have been more successful. I now realize I needed a mentor, which I highly recommend to my grandchildren. In a way Mr. John Pickell, my high school principal, was a part-time and unofficial mentor to me and would have been more accessible had I approached him more often for advice and guidance when I was uncertain about my future.

Later in life, I have come upon occupations that would have appealed to me had I know more about them, public service and collegiate athletic administration, for example. I think I have been always interested in helping people and being involved in such things as the Council on Aged and Aging in Greencastle, and I have become increasingly interested in politics as I read books in the past few months about the Clintons and others. Not that I ever aspired to be a major politician, but it has occurred to me that I would have enjoyed and been devoted as a member of the state legislature or a member of Congress if I were bright enough and clever enough to persuade people to vote for me.

Just a random thought: I hope my grandchildren will

understand the importance of setting goals and aspirations and begin pursuing them in whatever manner that suits their style and interests.

I don't think my parents were aware enough of guiding me in the directions that I should have been thinking about. And I don't think I have done a very good job of helping my own kids explore their interests or suggesting pursuable objectives sufficiently to capitalize on their best instincts and talents although I would like to think that the career objectives they have chosen are excellent and in line with the talents they have honed so well for themselves, which makes me very happy that they have apparently found a niche in life that fulfills their aspirations and desires and a sense of accomplishment. Sometimes I think about "Oh, there's a job, I'd like to have." But I realize it's too late now, so I think about my grandchildren and how they will face their future and how they will live it as a member of the work force, whatever their calling turns out to be.

I am thrilled that Emily, Cindy's daughter in Georgia, is pursuing nursing and knows that's what she wants to do; she extended her college career to pursue R.N. certification.

I think Grant is still mauling over how he wants to live his life in a fulfilling business career.

And I believe Chloe and Henry and Emma and Michael, all of whom are excellent students now in grade, middle and high school are sufficiently motivated, bright enough and, with parental guidance, will in time, identify the type of career that fits their needs and hopes so they'll have a career that pleases and rewards them in their adult lives. But they must give it some sober thought and planning and seek advice from others in their desired career fields. End of sermon.

It's difficult for me to recall the many facets of my time at DePauw. So I will simply call up some of my most vivid memories or events, conflicts or personalities that stand out in my mind. In 1975 President Kerstetter becme chancellor and was succeeded on an interim basis by a man named Tom Binford. Binford was named acting president and had been an Indianapolis bank president and a mogul at the Indianapolis 500 Speedway. Tom was a man you could call by his first name and I think I had his confidence. He appointed and promoted me to the position of Director of Public Relations, Editor of the Alumni Magazine with responsibilities to oversee the directors of the News Bureau and of Summer Conferences. I accepted the challenge with a salary of $18,000 with benefits, mostly tuition for my children.

I am writing now mainly from a stream of consciousness, rather than having a well-documented diary of activities for myself or my job. So I will record incidents or events or activities randomly as I recall them. Backing up somewhat from the mid 1970's it somehow entered my memory today of where we were when Neil Armstrong landed on the moon and first walked on the surface of that lonely, cold planet. Judy, the kids, and I were on a trip to the East, and were spending the night at a Holiday Inn motel in Bethlehem, Pennsylvania, where we stayed up through the night to watch in awe and pride to see Armstrong walk down the metal steps of the lunar lander to say "One small step for (a) man, one giant step for mankind" or something like that.

Some people, even in America, believed this did not actually happen, but was as they claimed a staged, bogus event. I seem to think we were on our way to New York City, where I was to attend the national convention of the American College Public Relations Society (ACPRA). I went to the daily meetings and Judy and the kids saw some of the sights of NYC. This trip to a convention was among several we took to summer conventions around the country. I recall interesting trips and conventions we made to Boston, to Miami, Florida, to Dallas, Texas, to Denver, Colorado, to Chicago and an extended summer trip in 1973, I think it was, to San Diego, in which we bought a cabin tent and camped all the way across the country, making stops in many states, while eating food that Judy had cooked at home and frozen for our use as we went from Greencastle, to stops in (I know some of the locations are incorrect as listed here, but my old memory fails me; I do know that we stopped at all of these places during some trip to the far west or the plains states(Springfield, Missouri, to Amarillo, Texas, to Gallup, New Mexico, and to Phoenix, Arizona) which we reached after a stimulating tour of the Grand Canyon, and then on to San Diego, where we stayed in a Motel 6. As I recall a particular fun picnic we had on the grounds of the Grand Canyon where, unobserved, I sprinkled coins in the dirt which we had covered with a cloth, and then pretended to find the coins to the delight and mystification of the kids, especially

55

Kurt who was about 7 at the time. I think they will recall that picnic too if I'm not mistaken. I also recall a trip to the Petrified Forest: Kevin was upset about something and refused to get out of the car, and also we had a warm and humid picnic at Papago Park in Phoenix on a hot day that the temp reached 109 degrees. I documented this three week trip that included a stop on the way home to visit with Jean Folk Walstrom, Judy's late sister, in Denver, Colorado. We also stopped at Four Corners where the borders of four states all converge to earn the title of *Four Corners*. The girls, Cindy and Kerry, also found jewelry there, made by native Americans. I think what they bought was turquoise jewelry. The kids seemed to enjoy or at least have fun living in the cabin tent which was about 15 feet long and about 8 feet deep. It was a bitch getting the tent out of the car or off the top of the luggage rack and taking time to erect it. Generally Kurt and Kevin helped with this project. I remember the day we left home that I had a terrible migraine headache that lasted most of the day. Also the second day we had set up the tent somewhere in Kansas and during the night a terrible rain and wind storm awakened us and we held on to the canvas of the tent to keep it from blowing away. In the morning we had to step around the puddles of water that remained from the rain storm. I have photos of the tent somewhere, perhaps they are among the items that I have stored at Kurt's house after my move from my condo in Camel to Sunrise, a retirement community in that city. I hope some day to get these slides transferred to video. During my sixth year at DePauw we were blessed with the birth of Kurt on January 23, 1966. Judy awoke at 5:30 a.m. on a cold, cold January morning with labor pains and thought she was calling Mrs. Stamper, who lived up by the DePauw observatory, to come down and stay with Kevin, Cindy and Kerry while she (Judy) and I went to the Putnam County Hospital. Instead of Mrs. Stamper, she incorrectly dialed another neighbor, Mrs. Floyd Peterson, and woke her up. But Mrs. Stamper, as I recall, did come and held down the fort while we were busy bringing our fourth child into the world, James Kurtis Aikman. It was now that we were so fortunate to have two boys and two girls in our family. Of course, they were beautiful, lovely babies and we took scads of photos of them over the years and love to step back and look at their development over the span of years. Thanks to my dear friend Ralph Taylor, who had his own photo studio and retail store uptown, we got many, many photos of our young family and these photos continued to be *gifts* to us from Ralph's generosity and time and trouble. I have already noted elsewhere that with Ralph's help I usually printed dozens of Christmas photos of our family and along with poetry or prose along with the photo to convey the Christmas message. I am proud of those often creative photos of my wonderful family and their diverse interests as reflected in the various photos. Other passing developments I recall but without much elaboration were these: I won't try to memorize all the stuff that happened or I was involved in at DePauw, and will only try to hit some of the high points that occur to me as being worth the retelling of them.

My office moved about five different times while I was spending my 27 years at DePauw. I started out in the basement of the Studebaker Administration building, then after some renovations, I moved into a paneled office on the second floor between that of my boss, Norman J. Knights, and Mike Carriker, the University's chaplain. Mary Hirt continued to be my trusty and capable secretary and we got along very well. She had a good sense of humor and I think I did, too.

I continued to report the news from DePauw to local, regional and national media. Although there were not too many stories that made the national media. One big philosophical/ideological issue that captured widespread interest occurred when the DePauw Board of Trustees voted to seek and accept Federal aid for the construction of what would be dedicated in 1972 as the Percy L. Julian Science and Mathematics Center. Percy was a noted chemist who was black and was raised in Greencastle after his family moved here from the South. He experienced a number of unfortunate racial incidents as a young man, however, and overcame this discrimination & rejection to develop a number of useful chemicals in his professional career. He even returned to DePauw to teach, but as I recall he was not given tenure because presumably of his race. I got to know Dr. Julian and he was a fine, gentle, bright and compassionate human being. The building that carries his name is one of the most imposing and dramatic buildings on the campus with its massive front pillars at the corner of College Ave and Hanna Streets. It was modified dramatically and expanded at a cost, I was told, of $40 million. I should mention that for several years I attended the meetings of the Board of Trustees, but somewhere along the line, I think it was when Dr. Richard Dick Rosser was president and an alumnus named Jim Kelly was chairman of the Board. They ceased inviting me to the meetings. I didn't take it personally, but it did make it difficult to determine what was newsworthy regarding the deliberations of the Trustees. I do recall that when Tom Binford came for about six months as an interim replacement for Dr. Kerstetter when he was abruptly named Chancellor of the University by chairman Stan Smith, that I was then attending the board meetings and put together a lengthy story which appeared in the Banner without any direction or vetting by Binford. Tom Binford complimented me on the solid story printed in the Banner about the actions of the Board of Trustees. I spent a good deal of time putting that story together without any input from "higher ups" as to what was appropriate to report to the public. Kerstetter would have wanted to read and edit and rewrite the story endlessly had he still been president. Binford seemed to trust my judgment and that gave me the impetus to write it as I heard and witnessed the actions of the Board. I always appreciated the candor of T.B. Mr. Smith was then chairman of the board of International Paper Company whose daughter Barbara would in time become my boss and with whom I did not particularly enjoy working.

Binford later asked me/appointed me to the new position of Director of Public Relations for DePauw, replacing the title of Director of the News Bureau. Though my duties just about remained the same, I did, however, address a bit wider spectrum of responsibility. I told Tom Binford, when he appointed me, that I didn't want to become an "apologist for DePauw." This was a needless observation from me and I don't know yet exactly I had in mind. But Binford, who was okay with this remark, was a down to earth, no nonsense businessman who had been acting head of the Indiana National Bank in Indianapolis and also chief steward of the Indianapolis Motor Speedway. So he had been around the track, so to speak and was one of Indianapolis' most respected citizens and *a shaker and a mover*. He was always informal and casual in his office. He would come into Greencastle and often pick up a lunch of something at a drive through restaurant and place it on the conference table in his office then get down to business. The only quirk in this entirely new arrangement was that my salary remained at $18,000. That was in 1975. When I eventually left DePauw in 1987 I was making about $42,000 per year. With this new title also came some more responsibilities—editor of the DePauw Alumnus magazine, overseeing the Summer Conference director's work and hiring Judy Magyar over the phone from South Africa, directing the work of John Maguley as director of the News Bureau, and directing the work of Greg Rice and Diane Phillips in Publications. Quite a different ball game, but all the people I worked with, including Brenda McBride, my secretary, and SID Bill Wagner, were people I liked and knew would do a good job for DePauw, and me.

I remember the first issue of the Alumni magazine I was

responsible for. A DePauw coed had recently won the title of Miss Indiana. We had a great photo of her in her queenly tiara and used a color photo of her on the cover. Shortly after that issue circulated philosophy professor Dr. Roger Gustavson stopped me on the street in downtown Greencastle one day and told me he thought that photo was inappropriate and had no business being on the cover of the magazine. I explained my rationale and said it was a considerable accomplishment for a DePauw student and brought substantial recognition to the kind of students we had at DePauw. It was not merely a swim suit competition but also included interviews, the contestants' goals in life and other types of questions that would or would not reflect an academic bent to the student's candidacy. We discussed the issue for some time and parted ways, I think, still as friends, or at least not adversaries. President Rosser was very supportive of me as he was during all of his years at DePauw on good or respectful terms. Dick, in fact, came over to my office in East College to compliment me, on the issue of the magazine mentioned above.

Dick was tickled, maybe *pleased* would be a better word, when one day he was riding his motorcycle down Locust Street. I was along the sidewalk with my camera and asked him if I could take a picture. He quickly obliged, pulling his safety helmet a little tighter, and I got the shot and took the film to Ralph Taylor. Ralph made a nice 11x14 and I gave it to Dick. He put it, now framed, on his office wall in a most conspicuous place. I always got along well with Dick Rosser and he was open to my suggestions and thoughts and advice. Dick was somewhat impulsive and I think he kept those around him hopping and always wondering what his next move or thoughts and plans would be. I know Bob Bottoms felt that and once made it known to me.

On the other hand, Dr. Kerstetter was very reserved and not outspoken nor did he have a buoyant personality as did Dick. The lone 'dustup' I had with Dr. Kerstetter was when a reporter, Jerry Footlick, from *Newsweek* magazine, came to campus to do a general story on campus moods around the county in the days when students were protesting everywhere. Jerry, who I had met on a media scouting trip to Washington D.C. where he was working at the time for the *National Observer*, and was introduced to me by DePauw alumnus Lee Dirks, '55, also a NO reporter at the time on the same trip. Jerry wanted to talk to some DePauw faculty ... so I arranged for him to meet for lunch with some moderate, candid faculty like Jim Gammon, Paul Kissinger and Bob Newton. I believe it was Old Gold Day and Dr. Kerstetter learned of the luncheon meeting in the UB and asked me if he should be meeting with the group. I don't remember how I avoided a candid explanation to him, but later that week I got a nice note from Dr. K saying he was pleased with the way Old Gold Day had come off. The reason I didn't want Dr. K. to meet Jerry was that I was afraid he would "spin" some overblown story about how serene DePauw's campus was and how devoid of protestations and student demonstrations it was.

That certainly wasn't the case and I wanted Jerry to see that we had nothing to hide and that I didn't want Dr. K. to gloss over these conditions, or the campus environment. This was not necessarily the way most PR people would have handled the situation, but I thought it was simply the honest way to deal with Jerry Footlick's visit. As it turned out his wrap up story on campus moods simply contained one sentence regarding what he found at DePauw, and it was neither good nor bad. I always found that if you weren't up front with the media on the first encounter it generally or often led to later difficulties or poor professional relations with the media, which we were always seeking to avoid.

I just finished a book about Hillary Clinton, *A Woman in Charge* by Carl Bernstein and it told throughout about the poisoned relationship between Hillary and the Washington media and later national media.

Regarding Footlick's visit, I did spend a number of days on various trips to Chicago, Washington and New York City calling on national media to whom I often took story ideas. I know that some actually produced a response, and I will cite a few here as substantiation. On a trip to New York City I dropped off a story idea about a new academic idea that offer tenured faculty a chance to explore a new type of career before retirement. My idea was about Tom Mont working on his sabbatical to earn a real estate license. NBC came to campus and did interviews with Tom and Dean Robert Farber about the novel program.

Another occasion came when I visited the *New York Times* to share a student organization's activity that included starting an emergency ambulance service, which later became a large, active county-wide service now called Putnam County Emergency Service/Operation Life. It all started with a group of creative, dedicated students. I got to know and exchanged communications & dinner invitations with Judy and me with the NY Times writer who came to campus to do that story. It was a PR plus for DePauw and the students, and as it turned out, Putnam County.

Another trip to New York to visit a network show, somewhat like CBS's 60 minutes, produced a visit from the show called "Sunday Morning." This story focused on the members of the undefeated, unscored upon 1933 DePauw football team that raised over $1-2 million to build the basketball fieldhouse in Lilly Center and to have it named after the team's football coach "The Gaumey Neal Fieldhouse." It was a great *feel good* story. Having the help of a professional group that assisted in "placing" such stories in the national media was very helpful in getting this particular story on national TV and the company that helped was based in Keene, N.H., whose employees became friends and professional advisers to me.

I also had some good luck in bringing *Sports Illustrated* to campus regarding the Monon Bell's colorful history. They came and covered the game with Wabash in the late 70's and did a well receive story on the tradition of this long-time series.

In the early 80's DePauw's men's basketball team ran up an incredible sixty two or sixty three home-game winning streak. I thought this was unusual and newsworthy. Furthermore the men's team collectively had a 3.0 grade point average, which was pretty unusual and a good academic angle so I put the story idea on the table for them, discussing the uniqueness of the winning record and the extraordinary team GPA. CNN sports liked the idea and sent a crew to Greencastle to do a TV story. Wouldn't you know it, the game they came to cover resulted in a loss, ending our 60 or so game winning streak. I felt this a big blow to the story and that the story would be killed, but they aired the story anyway and just used the action of the losing game with IUPUI as what they call B-roll footage. So it came off in a positive way after all and we got good exposure on this national cable network. Of course I also made frequent trips to Indianapolis to visit local TV stations, the wire services (AP and UPI) as well as *The Star* and *The News*, where I had made a number of professional friends through the years and through my membership in the Society of Professional Journalists/Sigma Delta Chi. Tom Keating was a particularly good friend and journalist who wrote a daily column for *The Star*. I often fed Tom potential human-interest off-beat ideas that he turned into neat columns relating news of and about DePauw and its students/staff. Tom was always a good, talented friend who wrote some very nice things about me professionally in his column. "He's (me) one of the best in the business." He wrote following my furnishing him a lead for a good human interest story from DePauw. Unfortunately, he died at a very young age of 45. About this time, while participating in the Indianapolis chapter of SPJ/SDX in Indy, I also worked with the chapter in moving the Indiana Journalism all of Fame from an under exposed location there to a major room in East College, which had been renovated in the early 1980s. I remember helping to move furniture and a conference table into the new Hall of Fame, where we had photos and plaques and displays of those who had been inducted in the annual ceremonies that were held in the DePauw Student Union Building. Now (2012) I understand that the SPJ/SDX chapter is thinking about moving the Hall of Fame to the Ernie Pyle Journalism Building at Indiana University. I'll be sorry to see it go if it does go. It was good for DePauw to have it here and to draw the state's practicing journalists to the campus on an annual basis to the Journalism Hall of Fame inductions. I worked with the national organization of SPJ/SDX to host the 75th anniversary of the society at DePauw, including some of the nation's top journalists, Jane Pauley, formerly of CBS's network show, TODAY, and many others whose names I have forgotten or never knew.

So many other memories of my days at DePauw are worthy of mention but I don't know where to begin, so I'll tackle it by randomly mentioning a few that stand out in my mind for one reason or another: because they were just plain fun and exciting or because there was something historic vis a vis DePauw.

One of the exciting and fun and fun things I did while at DePauw was making road trips with the basketball teams. The first big one was to New York City in about 1960 or so. We flew to NYC and played Fordham and then Army at West Point. We also made a stop in Hamilton, NY to play Colgate University. Elmer McCall, the head coach, was always kind and thoughtful to me and included me when it came time to have one's travel expenses paid. What I mean is that the University's Athletic Department picked up my tab as well as those of the players … my airfare, my meals and my housing. I never traveled with the football team, because I just did not have a close relationship with the coach, Tom Mont. Usually I drove to the football games, which we mostly played in Indiana. Frequently, the kids would go with me and often we would take a friend of one of them. Cindy liked to take Lisa Kissinger. Lisa also often went to the basketball games with us in old Bowman Gymnasium, replaced in 1981 by the new Lilly Center and its Gaumey Neal Fieldhouse, a gift of the 1933 DPU football team.

In the late 1970's I was authorized to have a full-time sports information director (SID) who handled the press and statistics for all the sports teams with emphasis on football and basketball. Bruce Ploshay, who had helped me keep stats during the two sports seasons (football and basketball) later worked part-time with Page Cotton, the basketball coach as an assistant and helped me with the SID work out of my office in East College. This was part of his work as a graduate student at DePauw. Bruce continued to play a role in my life. After he graduated from DePauw in 1975, he became a salesman for a chemical company in the East and did extraordinary work after having graduated with a major in chemistry. A few years later, Bruce, thinking he might want to become a basketball coach, returned to DePauw; that's when he helped with the work of an SID. I always enjoyed having Bruce around; everyone in my office liked Bruce, because he was energetic and full of ideas and anxious to act on them.

The year after Bruce came to help me, he moved over to the athletic department to help Page Cotton, today (May 2011) the Athletic Director of DePauw and more recently special assistant to President Casey.

Always moving up, Bruce then joined the Development Office in fundraising, becoming Director of Capital Gifts, if I remember correctly. I should also point out that because of my relationship with Bruce and his wife, Anne, they consulted me on purchasing houses, which they would modernize and renovate for resale. The first house I sold them was on South College Avenue then another just west of that site and then the final one on Seminary Street, a two-story house just around the corner from the Delta Tau Delta fraternity. They hired son Kevin to do some renovations for them. I owe a great deal to Bruce and Anne for allowing me to sell them houses and to relist them when they were ready to move on. My history with Bruce continued when I moved to Indianapolis in 2003, where they had moved several years earlier for Bruce to enter financial management. Most of the non-cash assets, except my farm, were placed under the management of Bruce and his associates. I always felt that Bruce and his colleagues went out of their way to help me or answer any questions that I may have had. Unfortunately, when some of the kids decided to have the court manage my financial affairs, all my tangible assets were turned over to a trust company in Indianapolis for management. This company was managed by a guy named George whatever, the most unapproachable and inhospitable guy I had ever encountered, *and to think he was working for me.* I'll never understand how this guy became part of my life, which I found deeply disturbing and hurtful and eventually impractical.

As of this day, as I write this account, I am still trying to figure out how to rid my life of this disgusting *businessman.* On the domestic scene, the kids were growing and expanding their experiences in school and life. They were making good grades in school, participating in some school activities (Kurt-sports/baseball; Kevin-theatre/organ restoration, lighting; Kerry-cheerleading and homecoming princess; and Cindy-tennis and a business internship & Kerry and Cindy-dating and Girl Scout cookie sales, in which they sold more than anyone else by hitting the campus fraternities where they sold over 100 boxes one season, as I recall, winning top prizes. Both the girls were dating regularly, Cindy to Russell Christian, whom she eventually married in June 1979; and Kerry, who dated Terry Gobert, for a number of years then broke up with him. I had the good fortune to be inducted into the DePauw Athletic Hall of Fame as an honorary member in 1998 and into the Indiana Basketball Hall of Fame in 2008 as the St. Vincent Silver Medal Winner, which made me a member of the Hall itself. This SVSM honor goes to a person for his or her contributions to Indiana High School basketball, an honor given me for my work with the Indiana All-Star Basketball Program as its Game Director from 1988-2007, sponsored by *The Indianapolis Star*. The Indiana

Basketball Coaches Association, directed by Steve Witty, ex-Ben Davis coach and two-time State champion, honored me in 2011 by naming one of their scholarships the Pat Aikman, Leadership and Character Award. I made the first two presentations at the Indiana-Kentucky All-Star games in Bankers-Life Fieldhouse in June 2012 in Indianapolis to a girl from Tipton and a boy from Bloomington. I also read the students' applications and made non-binding recommendations regarding the ultimate winners to Coach Witty. I hope this is not considered a conflict of interest, because I also worked for a year for Steve, recruiting sponsors for the IBCA.

I landed two sponsors and their sponsorship dollars from two major sponsors, The Indiana Pacers and Methodist Sports Medicine for the Coaches Association, to which I also belong. Another honor I received on September 14, 2001, as a result of "clandestine" work by Paul & Joanne Kissinger. They had arranged through friends in the State Government to have me receive what is called *The Sagamore of the Wabash* distinction, the highest civilian award given by an Indiana Governor. My honor was signed by Governor Frank O'Bannon, a Democrat from Corydon, Indiana. The award was presented to me by State Representative Susan Crosby from Roachdale, and by a long-time member of the State Senate Senator Connie Lawson, now Secretary of State, of Danville, Indiana. Judy and I were attending a Christmas party at the home of Dave and Lynn Bohmer, when the surprise announcement and presentation were made. I was totally floored when they told me about this honor and I was so pleased and grateful to Paul and Joanne, long-time good and thoughtful friends from my DePauw days. Paul, on behalf of the DePauw faculty for whom he was secretary, even wrote me a highly complimentary letter in which he praised me for my years of service to DePauw University. I liked the letter so much I will repeat its final paragraph here, pardon my possibly excessive pride in this Sept. 14, 1987, letter from the esteemed Secretary of the DePauw faculty:

"All of this adds up to an illustrious career built by a respected colleague whose quality performance, integrity, sensitivity and humor have made you a special friend to each of us (the faculty) at DePauw."

Signed: The Faculty of DePauw University (P.B. Kissinger, Secretary).

Judy and I had our ups and downs through these years and some wonderful trips, our first trip abroad to Europe in 1986—to England, the Netherlands, France, Switzerland, Italy, Germany and Belgium … a three-week tour that included two weeks on a TWA tour to all the tourist sites—Paris and the Eiffel Tower and the Mona Lisa in the Louvre; to Florence, Italy to see the sculpture of David, to Venice to ride in a man-powered gondola and to London to see Big Ben, Westminster Cathedral, and Buckingham Palace, and scores of other memorable sites. After our two-week TWA tour ended in Amsterdam, we rented a car and drove about 1120 KM around much of the Netherlands, France and Germany, stopping in Strasbourg and Freiburg, Germany, to visit sites where DePauw had study programs for its students. We also visited foreign friends, the Willy Kind's in Bamberg, Germany; Willy had lived with us during our first year at DePauw when he came to Greencastle as a Duisburg Fellow, a German exchange program directed by Dr. Hans Grueninger, on the DPU faculty and faithful advisor to my Phi Delt house. I am not sure I would tackle driving on my own through Western Europe again. Although we had no problems on the autobahns, we were often travelling at 80 mile per hour over unfamiliar territory. As I recall we only got lost seriously once as we were travelling around Nuremberg, Germany. We particularly had an interesting time in a Dutch town as we passed through while driving and saw Hotel DePauw. I told Judy we must stop, so we did and decided to stay the night there and have dinner with the owners' daughter. She told us she wanted to come to the U.S. with her boyfriend and find a job. I told her we would find out about a green card for her and her boyfriend, so when we got home I checked with the U.S. Government to find the regulations and sent the info to her.

Later in 1986 Judy decided to move out on her own, leaving me in the house at 801 Highwood. I am not sure why, but it was an almost ever present feeling she had, according to my recollection, that she wanted her freedom and I wasn't what she wanted in a husband, apparently, although, to my recollection she never told me precisely why she wanted to move out. I remember that on the particular weekend in November, 1986 I went to Cincinnati, if I recall accurately, while Judy's folks came down from Oak Lawn and helped her move into an apartment in a two-story white house on the corner of Seminary and Indiana streets, across the street from the present day (2011) Cinema and catty-corner from the Walden Inn. She lived there until July of 1987 and we agreed, during a conference on the patio of 801 Highwood that, she would return to 801 Highwood. As I recall, we continued to have a single bank account on which we both wrote checks. By then we owned two vehicles and pretty much went our own way as we have continued to do since we were divorced finally in Feb., 2003, in a development that surprised me.

This was the first of two short term separations. A few years later—and I don't remember the year now—she decided to move out again and the Morrills invited her to live in the apartment unit that belonged to the mother of one of them. It was in what they called Parkwood Village, just off Wood Street. I told Judy that I would trade places with her after a month, and so I moved into the Parkwood Village apartment for a month and then we reconciled and moved back in together in our original home. Over these years Judy worked in a number of jobs, mostly in social work for Headstart in Greencastle, then Spencer and Martinsville and finally in Brazil. Previously, she had helped start a clinic for poor people in around 1971 or 72 in the south part of Greencastle where free medical services were offered by Dr. Jimmy Johnson and Dr. Anne Nichols. Judy was director of the clinic and often did a lot of driving to pick up and deliver patients to and from the Health Clinic. She was a key factor in getting this program and service up and running.

She worked for several months as an unpaid volunteer. Later the clinic received a grant to help underwrite some of its expenses, including the services provided by Judy, who was, I recall, director of the clinic.

My civic work in the early 70's was as Vice President of the Putnam County Senior Center of which I was one of three co-founders with Louise Johnson and Dr. Rusty Elliott. My first assignment was to plan and execute the installation of an elevator in the Center. Mission Accomplished! I was also on Greencastle's Quality of Life Committee, chaired by DPU President Dick Rosser. I joined the Greencastle Kiwanis Club in 2012.

My leaving DePauw was not exactly what I would have hoped for. In mid-1987 Bob Bottoms, without any staff members' input or knowledge, hired Barbara Smith, the daughter of the chairman of the Board of Trustees Stan Smith, as something like VP for Advancement/Development or something like Asst. to the President, I don't recall exactly what her title was, except she was determined to do it her own way. She had been in the advertising and PR business in an agency in New York City, I guess. Barbara and I did not really mesh in terms of how we dealt with people and how we managed our jobs. We had a luncheon meeting one day in mid-summer 1987 and she did all the talking, and I found it an unpleasant lunch, although we did not argue. I just did not enjoy being in her presence and apparently she felt towards me the same way. At any rate, one day she asked me to come up to her office in Charter House. I'll never forget it. She told me she was going to put me on 90-day *notice* and would in the meantime evaluate my work and contributions. At this time, after having been made director of PR by Tom Binford in 1975, I was editor of the Alumnus Magazine, Director of PR, and managed the directors of the News Bureau, Summer Conferences(Gwen Bottoms) and Sports Information. It was abundantly clear to me that Barbara did not want me to continue working at DePauw. So I was willing to oblige her, after telling her I thought I had brought to DePauw many friends as a result of my professional and personal work and contacts, and I thought I had been exceedingly loyal to DePauw and effective in my job. It was painful to recollect those days because what she told me was crushing to my spirits at the time and made me bitter for awhile, towards DePauw and in particular Bob Bottoms, who waived any role in my relationship with Miss Smith. I did not speak to Bottoms for several months after this even though his wife Gwen had worked for me in the office. I did, of course, speak to Gwen.

After this showdown with Miss Smith, I scheduled an appointment with President Bottoms. I told him what she had told me, waiting and hoping for any kind of show of support or concern he might offer. He said to me, "You and Barbara are exact opposites – like oil and water. You need to work it out." I felt that he had no further loyalty to me at this point although he had given me the largest annual raise I had ever gotten at DePauw only a year or so earlier. It was clear to me finally that Bob either agreed with her and did expect us to "work it out." Just about everyone knows that oil and water do not mix effectively. It did not make sense for me to continue at DePauw even if I had been happy there. I loved my Alma Mater and I loved the work I was doing with the good people on my staff. Two of them left DePauw very shortly after.

I did not want to continue at DePauw in such a semi-hostile or unpleasant environment. So I began looking at other opportunities, although I could not see myself leaving an institution I loved and felt loyal to; however, if it were not a hospitable environment, I did not in any case wish to remain. Soon I saw an ad in a PR journal that Trinity University in San Antonio, Texas, was seeking a director of public relations. I checked it out and was encouraged to send my resume and references. Fortunately, I had a wonderful experience at Southern Methodist University, while on a one semester sabbatical in January-June 1987. Trinity's hiring officer contacted my host at SMU to secure useful information/references. They gave me a good recommendation and I was invited to San Antonio to interview for the job. The trip and visit were fine, I liked the institution and the professionals I met there. On the last day of my three day visit I was feeling deeply that I couldn't make the move to Texas and I told my host, Mark, that I couldn't make the move. He was very cordial and wished me well, telling me in the process that they had wanted to hire me. So I flew back to Indianapolis, feeling unhinged and desolate.

On the following weekend Judy and I drove to Oak Lawn, Illinois to see her folks and to spend some time up there. I had this constant feeling that I should reconsider my feelings about

Texas. And so I did, calling Mark, my contact, at Trinity asking if the job was still open. When he told me "yes," I asked if they still wanted to consider me and Mark said "yes" and invited me down to San Antonio to look for housing. Judy went with me on this trip and was ready to make the move. Cindy, our daughter, was in favor of it, because she was living in Dallas at the time and welcomed her parents to come to Texas. So we flew down to S.A. for three days of house-hunting and social events. I liked what I saw and the people I met and was impressed that Trinity was an even better institution that I thought DePauw was and I definitely liked the man, Mark, for whom I would be working and to whom I would be reporting. Yet, throughout the last two days I was there, I had this terrible panic attack, that prevented me from feeling at ease and comfortable with my prospective new employer, Trinity U. So when Mark came to pick Judy and me up to take us back to the airport to return to Indiana, I had to tell him, "I am very sorry, but I just can't make this move." My heart was definitely telling me I wanted to stay in Indiana or very close-by. Mark was surprised but didn't force the issue, which made me happy. We flew back to Indianapolis and I was greatly relieved but was obviously still uncertain what my future held. I had already submitted my resignation to Dr. Bottoms and given the Greencastle *Daily Banner* a story about my new employment in Texas. Not long afterwards I received a call from Jim Baker, president and chairman of the board of Arvin Industries in Columbus, Indiana. Jim was also a DePauw trustee and his wife, Bev, had been in a class of mine. Jim asked me to come to Columbus to interview for the position there as director of investor relations. So I drove the two hour trip to Columbus and went through the interview process and the salary discussion. I was offered the job at a salary of $52,000, about $10,000 more than I was making at DePauw, which I had just left. I came home to consider my future and that of my family.

At this time, a friend of mine who was working at DePauw as Director of the Media Center, Drake Mabry, former newspaper editor from Des Moines, IA, told me that I was welcome to use an office in his building to pursue my job opportunities. This was certainly a very generous gesture by Drake and I accepted it, moving into an office in what was initially the old Delta Zeta house on Anderson Street, just out the back of the Administration Building. Drake made his secretary, Carol Waltman, available to me as well as my own phone and desk. I think about the irony now of the situation. Before I made a final decision I answered an ad in the paper for a director of PR at IU's regional campus in Kokomo. I drove up there and went through interviews, but quickly decided to take my name out of the mix. I had been spoiled by the environment and type of people I knew at DePauw with certain exceptions.

Finally after dithering for a few more weeks I called Jim Baker and thanked him for the opportunity with Arvin Industries and told him I was going to take a job with *The Indianapolis Star* as promotion coordinator, which I started on Jan. 25, 1988.

I was to replace a man, Don Bates, who had been with *The Star* for some years, but apparently had a difference of opinion with his boss, Jim Pauloski, who would be my kind and engaging boss for the next 19 years.

I had learned of *The Star* job through a friend, Bo Connor, who was *The Star*'s editor, and who had a son on the DePauw basketball team. On my first day at *The Star*, Jim took me around to many offices and introduced me to many of the people I would be working with. I felt as though he was really proud of my joining his staff and I came to really like and respect Jim, even though we had different perspectives on some of the assignments and special events that I was to deal with. My new job, at which I started at $37,000 a year, much less than I had been making at DePauw and $15,000 less than what I would have made at Arvin, entailed writing promotional ads that previewed coming stories or events that would be appearing in *The Star*'s news pages or promoting events which *The Star* sponsored. In taking this job, two of my personal needs were met. I would enjoy, I knew, the special events in which I would be engaged—the Indiana-Kentucky High School All-Star basketball games—played for charity each summer, the Jefferson Awards to outstanding and largely unrecognized volunteers. So ... I was following my heart, so to speak and I would continue doing something I really liked and enjoyed with colleagues I would come to like very much. And I would continue to live in Greencastle although I would become a regular commuter of nearly 100 miles roundtrip a day, which did not become a big issue with me.

There was always something new going on with *The Star*, and you didn't have to conjure up ideas of events to make the job challenging and fun. It was a real pleasure to meet new professionals both in our department and in the general news/editorial and sports departments. This was before Gannett, the giant newspaper chain, purchased *The Star* and *The News* and then killed *The News*. Many people complain to me about how "thin" *The Star* is presently. I would guess that the revenue there has dropped considerably. Much of the thinness of *The Star* is due to fewer ads of all types, and staffing at the paper has been reduced, perhaps more than I realize. My major complaint with *The Star* has been trifling, but I was very disappointed in the failure of the Sports Editor to note the remarkable successes of the DePauw women's basketball team. "You are not in our marketing area," they tell me. Then why do they try to sell subscriptions in Putnam County? Technology has also changed the priorities of newspapers everywhere, in my opinion. When I read *The Star* or Greencastle's *Banner Graphic* I want a hard copy I can sit down with at Starbucks and read the issue from cover to cover. But I realize no newspaper meets all the needs and fancies all of its readers all of the time.

I retired from *The Star* job of promotion coordinator in 2000, but continued as game director of the Indiana All-Star event with Kentucky until September 2007.

Two

Photo Memories

The author, son Kurt, Carmel, Indiana, former wife Judy, and grandson Michael Aikman.

Son-in-law Ron Michalak and daughter(Ron's wife) Dr. Kerry Gayle Aikman, grandchildren Henry and Chloe Michalak of Edina, Minnesota.

J. Patrick Aikman

Grandson Grant Robinson, Atlanta, Georgia.

Brother Mike Aikman and his wife Shielda, Terre Haute.

Author, daughter Cindy Robinson, granddaughter Emily, former wife Judy and Tim Ebbinghouse, Cindy's significant other, Atlanta, Georgia.

Granddaughter Emily DeCesare, and husband Blake DeCesare, Valdosta, Georgia.

Front: Late sister-in-law Jean Wahlstrom, her husband David, and her brother Robert. In Back: Former mother- and father-in-law Evelyn and Vincent Folk, Oak Lawn, Illinois.

Former wife Judy Aikman and son Kevin, Vienna, Austria.

Author's parents Charlotte and Herbert Aikman, Dana, Indiana.

Author hoisted up by sophomore teammates to cut down net as a result of winning Dana High School's annual Class Basketball Tournament.

J. Patrick Aikman

7th grade basketball team at Dana, the Cobras. Author is in the middle of the back row.

Sophomore boys, upset winners of annual high school basketball tourney. Front: Volunteer coach Jack Hendrix, Pat Aikman, Eddie Scott: Standing left to right: David Roe, Dale Hess, Charles Blue, John Cook, Robert Harrington, William Potter, Jimmy Marshall.

Author displays blue ribbon won in county track meet for 50-yard dash in 1950.

Author as 7th grade power forward.

The author (right) presents the Pat Aikman Character and Leadership Scholarship to students from Bloomington and Tipton at the 2012 Indiana-Kentucky All-Star games in Indianapolis at Banker's Life Fieldhouse. Awards given by the IBCA's executive director Steve Witty (left).

Pat's cousin Lynda Thompson Profitt, Dayton, Ohio and Pat Aikman in Dana.

Pat's maternal grandmother Violet Shepherd Jones, near her country grocery store, the Jot 'Em Down in Logan, Illinois.

Author's gathering of friends at a Christmas party with former wife Judy. Friends are: The Grays, the Morrills, the Jacksons. the Coopers, the Newtons, the Aikmans, Nick Steele, Cynthia Cornell, Walker Gilmer, and Joanne Kissinger.

Pat's first car, a black 1948 Pontiac, purchased for $1,200 in 1951.

My public relations and publications staff at DePauw. Back row, left to right: Dian Phillips, publications; Pat Aikman, PR; Joanne Kissinger, publications. Front row, left to right: Brenda McBride, office manager; Greg Rice, publications; Judy Magyar, summer conferences, at staff picnic in Greencastle's Robe-Ann Park. Not pictured; Bill Wagner, Joe Owens and Bruce Ploshay, sports information directors; John McGauley, news bureau; Linda Allee, secretary; Marian Maloney, publications; Eunice Martindale, publications; and Char Alexander, publications. Gwen Bottoms, summer conferences, and Bert Anderson, publications. These colleagues did not all work during the same years. (Photo courtesy of Greg Rice)

J. Patrick Aikman

DePauw's Studebaker Administration Building. Author's office is on second floor, middle three windows.

A traditional Aikman Christmas Card. The kids are (left to right) Kerry Gayle, James Kurtis, Cindy Sue and John Kevin.

Decorative monument donated by alumni, marking the spot where Dana High School once proudly stood until it was razed in the early 1960's to make room for a town park on the former school grounds.

Dana High School had its own afghan created, thanks to classmate Wanda Berry Samford.

Dana High School Class of 1953 skips meal at Mag's Restaurant in Dana to dine at the Royale Cafe in D.C , accompanied by Principal John Pickell and his wife, Alice, and B&O rep seated.

Dana High School Class of 1953 in Terre Haute train station, preparing to start Senior Trip to Washington, D.C.

One of the author's favorite teachers, Mrs. Chloe James, who taught English and urged her students to remember poems and pithy quotations.

Author Pat Aikman delivered school valedictorian's address and receives his diploma from former Dana principal Ward Beanblossom.

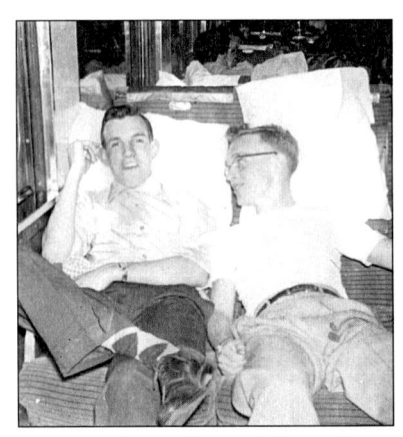

Pete Hatcher, right, and the author, are relaxed and seem to be having a good time, once on the train, headed to Washington, D.C. in the spring of 1953 – their senior trip.

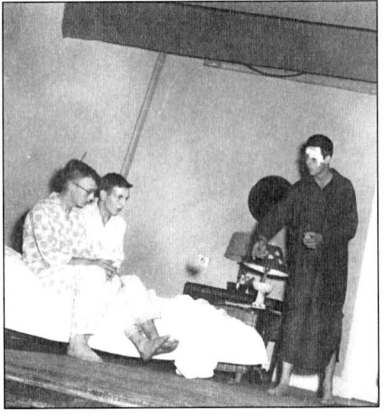

Pete Hatcher, left, and author, center, respond to classmate thespian Dale Hess in junior class play, Finders Creepers, in 1953.

Author's home from 1942-1957. This farm and house were the homestead for many generations of Aikman's. It was built circa 1910, 2.5 miles south of Dana, Indiana on State Road 71.

First home in 1957 of newly married Pat & Judy Folk Aikman on Main Street in Dana. Occupied 2nd floor rented apartment owned by the Rolland Ammerman family.

Second home in 1958 in Dana, two blocks east of Main Street. Previously owned by Pat's Auntie Dolleye Aikman Kerns.

First home the author and his family moved into when they left Dana, 45 miles eastward to Greencastle in 1960. The home is located at 7 Park Street, one block from the couple's alma mater, DePauw University.

J. Patrick Aikman

This house was built in 1962 by DePauw alumnus Bob Bruce for Pat and Judy and their children, Kevin, Cindy and Kerry, one block from DePauw's McKim Observatory at 801 Highwood Ave. They added a 5th bedroom and bath and other space in 1969 after the birth of James Kurtis. The home was sold in 2011.

For several generations the Aikman's, including the author and his parents, attended this small rural United Methodist Church in the crossroads community of Bono on State Road 71, a mile from his birthplace.

Memoirs of a Life

Main Street in Dana, looking north, circa 1930s and 1940s. A very unfortunate fire burned several of the buildings to the ground, including The Dana Theatre, in about 2005. On the immediate left today (2013) is the Ernie Pyle State Memorial Museum, honoring the life of this former Dana citizen, who distinguished himself as a Pulitzer Prize-winning correspondent during World War II and wrote at least four books about his experiences during the war. Friends of Ernie Pyle now staff the museum which was opened by the State of Indiana when the birthplace of Pyle was moved into Dana in 1976. The Museum is open by appointment by calling 765-665-3666.

Citizens of Dana meet in their only community gathering spot, the Dana Firehouse, to discuss the upcoming Ernie Pyle Fall Festival, staged in early August by community volunteers.

The Welcome to Dana sign touts the Ernie Pyle Memorial Museum while in the distance on the town's edge is an $18 million building project under construction on the local central grain elevator owned by the mega Cargill Company of Minneapolis.

Author Pat Aikman in a rare shot of him in his U.S. Air Force uniform when he served 11 months on active duty with his Air National Guard squadron in Terre Haute, during the Cuban Missile crisis. Scores of NG units were activated in 1961 by Pres. Kennedy when it appeared the Soviet Union and the US would clash over the Soviets' attempt to place rockets in Cuba.

Author's mother, Charlotte Jones Aikman, enjoys the birthday cake set before her on her 90th birthday at the Walden Inn/Inn at DePauw, four months before her passing in April 2001.

The author's paternal grandmother and poet, Gertrude Aikman, relaxing on a handy garden bench. In left photo, with a jaunty dust cap and apron on, she harvests produce from her vegetable garden in Dana several decades ago.

When Vice President Richard Nixon came to the DePauw campus in 1957 Pat Aikman, on the right, was invited to interview him, along with a student from the campus radio station, WGRE; Aikman represented the campus newspaper as editor of The DePauw.

Pat's second encounter with a presidential candidate came in the spring of 2008 when he met then candidate Barack Obama at his church, St. Luke's United Methodist Church in Indianapolis and obtained his autograph.

Pat Aikman gives his cherished Phi Delt housemother Grace Gibney a big hug prior to his graduation from DePauw in 1957.

Pat's parents, Herbert and Charlotte Aikman, surround their son before attending graduation exercises at DePauw.

Home to Pat from 1953 to 1957 was the Phi Delta Theta fraternity at DePauw. He was vice president of the house his senior year.

Three Aikmans and Three Buicks, including Pat's first new car, a 1956 Special his parents delivered to him when he was a junior at DePauw. Brother Mike is at the rear of the trio, father Herb is in the middle, and Pat is in the front with his two-tone vehicle.

Dale Bracey, from Caruthersville, Missouri, was Pat's roommate in the Phi Delt fraternity for two years. Dale is now a retired Presbyterian Minister in California.

Judy Folk Aikman relaxes with her father-in-law Herbert Aikman on the massive porch swing on the Aikmans' broad porch as the spirea bushes bloom in the foreground.

Like Pat, Judy Folk was a 1957 graduate from DePauw. She came to Dana to visit often during the summer of 1957. They were married a few months later in suburban Chicago.

Mike, on the right, accompanies the author as they look in the Aikman front yard for a skunk that showed up briefly.

Pat's Uncle Leo leans against what is probably a Civil War cannon at the Kennesaw Mountain National Park outside Marietta, Georgia, where Leo was initially a curator and then later became a columnist for the Atlanta Constitution and Journal and a popular after dinner speaker.

Aunt Ira Aikman from Marietta, Georgia holds the reins of the Aikman boys' favorite pony, Old Buster, while Mike and Pat hold steady in the saddle.

Mike and Pat Aikman are ready to get a ride from Mike's horse, Pal, as they are hitched up for a ride in a large-wheeled training cart.

The author (right) and his first cousin John Harvey Parkay, who shared many happy experiences in and around Logan and Dana together.

Judy's father, Vincent D Folk, walks three of his grandchildren to church in Oak Lawn. The group includes, left to right, Kerry Gayle, Grandpa Folk, Cindy Sue and Kevin Aikman.

Aunts galore in Dana, left to right, the author, Ira Irby Aikman, Carrie Aikman Taylor, Dolleye Aikman Kerns, Ollie James Amis, all aunts are deceased.

Teenage granddaughter Emma Nicole Aikman of Carmel, Indiana.

The gold leather ball that was featured in 1989 during the 50th anniversary of the first All-Star team. The ball is signed by Indiana hoops greats Rick Mount, Bobby Plump, Judy Warren, Oscar Robertson, Kyle Macy, Jimmy Rayl, Hallie Bryant, Jason Garner, Teri Rosinski, Steve Alford, Dick and Tom Van Arsdale, Vicki Hall, Sharon Versyp, and many more.

The four Aikman children enjoy an unrestrained jolly time on a swing set in an unidentified city park in Louisville, Kentucky. They are (left to right) Kerry Gayle, Cindy Sue, James Kurtis, and John Kevin.

Three

Indiana All-Star Tidbits

I THINK THE MOST ENJOYABLE ASPECT OF MY work at *The Star* was managing and making decisions relative to the presentation of the Indiana High School All-Star basketball games, played against the best of Kentucky's high school players. The All-Star games were begun in 1939 by *The Star*. The first year the Indiana All-Star boys' team played the 1939 Indiana State high school championship team from Frankfort, coached by renowned coach Everett Case, later head coach at North Carolina State. My job as game director for *The Star* was multi-faceted. It involved selecting the players for both the boys and girls teams, selecting the head and assistant coaches, purchased uniforms and shoes and other required or needed gear like t-shirts, socks, and other accessories that promoted the event, like hats, etc.

I had never attended the All-Star games, which had been played vs. Kentucky since that series began in 1940 and has continued each year since except for the World War II years of 1943 an 1944. So the rivalry had a great history and I was to become part of it.

I had, of course, heard of this series, but never attended any of the games, which were usually played in Indianapolis and, as I was to discover, all over Kentucky, starting during my initial exposure in Louisville in Freedom Hall. Since I had begun my work at *The Star* in January 1988; the high school basketball season was well underway. Judy and I drove to Louisville to check out the venue there and to check out some potential hotels in that area where the players could be housed when we went down there for the games. Because I knew nothing of the prospective players who would ultimately be chosen for the Indiana teams, I needed to scout as many games and players as possible to become properly informed. I found this element of the job to be most enjoyable, traveling around the state to towns I had never visited and to gymnasiums I had never seen. The first two trips I made were to Benton Central High School to watch the girls' sectional which had two female players who would become prospects. On this trip I went alone in my 1983 Toyota pickup. The second game Judy went with me to a small town in Indiana to see a player who was a pretty highly touted guard, who had signed to attend a Division I program. I thought the kid seemed to be rather erratic, which surprised me. Little did I realize this omission would bite me in the butt later on when the team was announced. The way I determined the best players in the State at this time was by sending out a ballot to all the state's men's and women's coaches. They were asked to list their choices for the 12 best men, and the female team coaches were asked to list the 12 best woman players. I think we sent out 600 or so ballots, which also asked those voting to recommend deserving coaches who would ultimately become the teams' coaches during the two-week All-Star camp. A major and important part of my job became soliciting donors or sponsors of such things as uniforms, shoes, meals, travel means, and assorted other elements that would reduce the expenses of the games and yield more funds for our charity, which at that time was *The Star*'s Fund for the Blind. At the time I came to *The Star*, previous games had amassed over $1,000,000 in funds for the Blind Fund, which was used to support services for those who were blind, mostly providing access to an Indianapolis radio station that catered to blind or sight-impaired people who could not read a newspaper and thus got their news from the radio. We also funded some services at an Indianapolis not for profit company that hired blind or sight-impaired people and also provided some money to the Indiana School for the

Blind on the north side of Indianapolis. The recipient of the money we raised for charities eventually evolved to a wider group of not for profits which provided many different kinds of services in the Indianapolis area. I think the significant impact of our fundraising was greatest when we gave the money to support the blind. I met many fine people who served on the board of the Blind Fund. By the time I finished my work with the All-Stars the summer of 2007 we had raised approximately $1 to $1.5 million dollars additionally beyond what had been raised prior to my coming aboard. Our best one-year effort was just under $150,000. My first year with the program –1988 – our games and related activities netted around $68,000, which exceeded the previous year's total. So we got off to a flying start by surpassing the previous year's income. That was important to me to show that I could manage an event equally as successful if not more successful than my worthy predecessor, Don Bates, who moved from my department down to the Sports Department. Don and I became friends and he was often a mentor to me. What I learned that first year was that there were many fine, helpful coaches around the State who were willing and anxious to help me. It was my impression, reinforced by comments from friends/coaches that the All-Star games were considered to be a sort of *closed operation*, which did not want or did not welcome opinions from others outside the newspaper. This was reinforced for me by a friend/coach Tom May from Crown Point who had coached the All-Star girls' team and had won a couple of state championships. The term

I heard most often was that selection of the All-Star teams was "always political." This charge burned me up and I would ask sometimes what it meant that they were "always political." I think the thinking was that choices were made for some personal reason by myself or by the coaches or the newspaper people who were involved.

I can categorically say that I never made a choice for either team that was made for any reason other than the quality of the player. I have been subjected to overtures from individuals who badly wanted a friend or a family member, or God-daughter perhaps, placed on the All-Star team—even gestures from a player's prospective college coach might call and politely point out the merits of one of his or her recruits who would "make a great Indiana All-Star." But these cases are every rare, and it wasn't as though I was without access to regular media reports of where a player was going to continue his or her education at a specific college or university. Occasionally a player might delay announcing their college choice, thinking it might adversely affect their chance of becoming an All-Star.

We had players who were going to attend Division III schools who *got a good look* if the coaches and I thought they had the skills they should possess to be an Indiana All-Star.

One year a girl from near Indianapolis made a great show of her defensive skills during an exhibition game at Greenfield which my coaches and I scouted. She became an All-Star. She ultimately played on a national championship team in college.

Speaking of scouting, I learned a great deal about

the geography of Indiana and its cities and towns and gymnasiums. I traveled hundreds of miles during basketball season visiting such communities and gyms as Brownstown, Mt. Summit, New Harmony, South Putnam, Springs Valley, Lapel, Taylor, Northfield, Speedway, Boonville, Tipton, Tri-Central Valparaiso, Gary West, East Chicago Central, Bicknell, Martinsville, Fort Wayne, New Palestine, Elkhart, New Albany, White River Valley, Center Grove, Frankfort, Connersville, Fountain Central, Cloverdale, Bellmont , Brown County, Warsaw, Seymour, and Delta These were over a period of years and not in a single year, I also attended sectionals, regionals, semi-states and virtually all of the State Finals in Indianapolis. Being from a small high school myself, I like the Class System for one reason, getting to see unknown players, to me at least. Beau Bauer of 2ACass and Brody Boyd of 1A Union/ Dugger, although I was aware of Brody's skills, but I hadn't seen Beau until the State Finals. My point is if you are really All-Star material, you will be discovered; it may take a season or two, but not to worry. I know that Charlie Hall from Kokomo, a great, thoughtful guy who is now the Game Director, will be on your trail.

These pages, I originally devoted to dealing with some individuals' defections or dismissals on essentially the boys Indiana All-Star teams, but one of my two sons, after reading my initial manuscript, said, "Dad, why don't you talk about the positives of your experiences with the All- Stars rather than the negatives."

"Good point!" I thought. But I thought I probably owed it to any readers of this book with the expectations that I would reveal the manner and details of which certain male All-Stars left the team of their own accord or those who after being named to the teams, during their senior year, decided for reasons of their own not to compete for a spot on the squad or were dismissed for reasons only they know or which the All-Star coaches of that year and myself, the author of this book, have a few of the answers. So, I am not going to go into those issues here. Clearly, these kinds of interactions and responses did not happen with the girls' teams. Not during my 19 years dealing with the Indiana All-Stars.

The only occasion I recall was a two-hour meeting one night at 1 a.m. in the lobby of the Holiday Inn Hotel on the south side of Indianapolis with two girls, one of whom was seriously unhappy with her playing time earlier in the evening at Market Square Arena. The unhappy girl said, "I know the only reason I was chosen for the All-Star team was that I am black. I pointed out to her that she had a scoring average at a large northern high school that exceeded 20 points per game and that she was preferred by a large number of voters among the media and women's high school coaches who voted. I did recognize that there seemed to be very few accomplished black girls playing during my first few years with the All-Stars. There were none on my first girls All-Star team in 1988 and only two in 1989 and two in 1990. I felt that basketball fans in Indiana expected the All-Star team to include the 12 or 13 best players in Indiana to be on that year's team. There were, of course, those who felt there was discrimination against black girls those years, although we were always carrying four or five or six African-American kids on the boys team each year ... as we should have been.

The second All-Star girl who sat in on that late night discussion was ultimately to be a member of the Indiana Fever WNBA team in Indianapolis. I cannot begin to tell you how many people who told me – probably uninformed about the fact that the final All-Star decisions were made by myself with the advice of the coaches – that the process of selecting the team was "always political."

I believe the thinking was that choices were made for some personal reason by myself or by the coaches or you had to have a connection with the game director or until my last year with *The Star*. I always got weary of hearing people say the choices were a result of "political connections." To people who said this I always asked what do you mean that it's *"always political?"* I usually got a feeble response.

The Indiana Basketball Coaches Association is now managing the game. The Indianapolis Star has a hand in handling the promotion and advertising for the event. When you see the huge full page ads about the games' dates, pictures of the players and instructions about how to buy tickets, understand that that is the contribution The Star makes to the success of the games and how important that is to informing the public and selling the tickets each year.

There were a few changes I made during my 19 years as game director. On the whole, I believe they were useful and expanded the opportunities for high school players.

Up through 1995 we were paying *a sports entrepreneur* a good bit of money to assemble men's and women's adult teams (usually recent college graduates) to play the All-Stars around the state in exhibition games. The hope was that the All-Star teams would get a good test before the games with Kentucky. I asked he Sports Entrepreneur what he thought about creating a Junior All-Star team. He didn't think it was a good idea. I then went to Bobby Cox, at the IHSAA who was at that time handling issues related to basketball. "Is there any reason we can't have a Jr. All-Star team and play the Senior All-Stars in exhibition games?" Bobby said he saw no reason we shouldn't do that. So we did, creating a Core group of 6 players who would play in all exhibition games. Six more players to be named from Northern Indiana and 6 more from Southern Indiana The Core 6 would be joined by another 6 depending of what part of the state the exhibition games were to be played in. In my opinion the setup has worked well. Eighteen more girls and 18 more boys have the opportunity to show their stuff to fans around the state. The income from the exhibition games has grown by my last count substantially with a large crowd at Purdue when we played in Mackey Arena one year and had a gate of nearly $9,000. Other game sites have ranged from $2,000 and up. The players each year are selected by a group of coaches who are members of the Indiana Basketball Coaches Association. The Junior All-Star candidates now look forward to the teams' selection announcement almost as much as the senior All-Stars anticipate who will be selected for the Indiana teams that play Kentucky.

Selecting coaches for the All-Star teams was also an annual task and I worried each spring about making the right or best decision regarding who would be leading the teams in a particular year. I realized that the two-week job involved travel expenses, time away from one's vacation from school. And family disruptions as well and the prospective coaches' concern about winning the games and having a positive experience with the players.

In my 19 years with the All-Star games I had only two occasions in which high school coaches passed on the opportunity/job to coach the Indiana All-Stars. One had a conflict with a summer job and another said he was simply exhausted from the preceding season's demands and duration. Both were from Northern Indiana and I feel both would have done a good job with those year's All-Stars. Both had considerable success in their schools. One prospect turned down the job as an assistant coach to sign on as head coach the following year. Another coach turned down the head coaching job and instead wanted to serve as an assistant coach. Except for the first two years as game director, in 1988 and 1989, I had one head coach and one assistant. In 1989 one of my coaches suggested it would have been useful. to have had another assistant, so in 1990 I added a second assistant coach and that policy continued for my last 17 years. One thing I did learn after my first year, which surprised me, was that the women's coach had been paid less than the men's coach the year before I took over in 1988. All coaches in 1988 were paid the same sum, according to the level they served. Head coaches made $400 plus room, board and meals for a two-week commitment.

From time to time, when we sent out the ballot to vote on players for the girls and boys teams, I asked those coaches who received the ballot if they were interested in coaching the All-Stars. Many said "yes." Unfortunately, I could not hire such a flood of willing volunteers; I am sure many coaches were perplexed by the unextended invitation after they had volunteered.

Like players, ardent All-Star watchers like to see All-Star coaching assignments spread around the state. I was acutely aware of this pre- disposition. In reviewing the All-Star program from my last year, 2007, I found we had more coaches from the southern part of the state than we did from either the central or northern parts of Indiana.

Boys Coaches from the South

Jim Miller, New Albany; Dan Bush, Bedford North Lawrence; Bill Stearman, Columbus North; Jack Butcher, Loogootee; Gene Miiller, Vincennes Lincoln; Joe Hinton, Floyd Central; Dave Clark, White River Valley; John Heaton, Shelbyville; Mike Broughton, Jeffersonville; Mel Siefert, Batesville; Howard Renner, Connersville; Mike Brown, Paoli; Will Wyman, Evansville Harrison; J.R. Holmes, Bloomington South; Jim Matthews, New Washington; Steve Brunes, Castle;

Bryan Hughes, Barr-Reeve; Tom Beach, Forest Park; Jim Shannon. New Albany; Steve Brett, Loogootee; Jerry Bomholt,, Shawe Memorial.

Girls Coaches from South

Donna Sullivan, Seymour; Rick Marshall, South Knox; Jed Beatles, Pike Central; Bob Howe, Jennings County; Lori Robbins, Connersville; Lisa Cook, Silver Creek; Mel Good, Columbus East; Angie Hinton, New Albany; Karen Stenfenagle, Jasper; Bruce Dockery, Evansville Memorial; Donna Cheatham, Southwestern; Debbie Marr, Columbus North; Walt Raines, Franklin; Larry Pringle, Triton Central; Marty Niehaus, Forest Park.

Boys Coaches from the North

Ron Heflin, Gary Roosevelt; Jim Hahn, Concord; Steve Austin, So. Bend St. Joseph; Jim Hammel, Lafayette Jefferson; Bill Patrick, Whitko; John Todd, E.Chicago Central; Al Rhodes, Warsaw; Jim East, Merrillville; Marty Johnson, East Noble; Dean Foster, Elkhart Central; Joe Otis, LaPorte; Dan Gunn, Northwood; Mike Drews,Elkhart Central; Pat Skaggs, Benton Central; Bob Punter, Valparaiso; Cliff Hawkins, Dekalb; Wayne Barker, Bluffton; Chris Benedict, Columbia City.

Girls Coaches from the North

Wayne Kreiger, Columbia City; Jan Conner, Benton Central; Will Wienhorst, Warsaw; Dave Riley, Ft. Wayne Northrop;

Tom May, Crown Point; Fred Fields, Huntington North (2); Greg Kirby, Valparaiso (2); Mike McCroskey, Kokomo; Tom Megeysi, Lake Central; Dan Burton, McCutcheon; Renee Turpa, Portage; Cindy Lester, Western; Mike Hey, Leo; Kevin Brown, North Judson; Charlie Hall, Kokomo; Teri Rosinski, Ft. Wayne Luers; Jack Campbell, Chesterton; Kathy Layden, Tri-Central; Kim Bilskie, Twin Lakes; Chris Huppenthal, Highland; Marilyn Coddens, So. Bend Washington.

Girls Coaches from the Central part of the State

Tom Earlywine, Mt. Vernon-Fortville; Linda Barnett, Clinton Central; Judie Warren (2) Carmel; Bob Kirkhoff, Roncalli; Mike Griffin, Brownsburg; Stan Benge, Ben Davis; Mike Armstrong, Perry Meridian; Joe Lentz, Center Grove; Linda Bamrick, Cathedral; Connie Garrett, Clinton Prairie; Tracy Hammel, Lebanon; Denise McClanahan, Southport; Jodie Whitaker, Lawrence North; Jon Howell, Alexandria-Monroe; Haley Beauchamp, Hamilton Southeastern; Julie Shelton, Mt. Vernon-Fortville;Todd Salkowski, Shenandoah; Curt Bell, New Castle

Boys Coaches from the Central part of the State

Pat Rady, Terre Haute South; Ed Siegel, Pike Twp; Bill Springer, Southport; Jimmy Howell, Mt. Vernon-Fortville; Jack Keefer, Lawrence North; Steve Witty, Ben Davis; Garth Cone, Alexandria-Monroe; Bob Heady, Carmel; Mark James, Franklin Central; Jim Jones, Terre Haute North; Larry Nicks, Arlington;

Dave McCullough, Noblesville; Chip Mehaffey, Winchester; Mark Barnhizer, Perry Meridian; Joe Buck, Pendleton Heights; Steve Bennett, New Castle; Mike Miller, Lawrence Central.

    Some have either retired, changed schools or careers.

    Negative behavior or big egos did not surface with the girls team, but it did with the boys from time to time. I recall 3-4 episodes. I usually named the team in April. A boy called me in May to say he would not be available for the Kentucky games. He was dropped from the team. Another year a boy became upset that he was subbed for and refused to sit on the bench. After the game he gave the media an ill-advised piece of his mind about his experience and quit the team; his mother asked me to reinstate him. I refused. The third case involved a boy who was pulled from the game during a hometown appearance. He was angry and refused to join his teammates in the halftime locker room; his teammates voted that he was a distraction to the business at hand. He was dismissed from the team. As 2013 All-Star Coach Scott Heady said about his team and others, "In a lot of All-Star experiences, coaches have a difficult time with egos, playing time and who gets the shots. We just didn't have to deal with that (in 2013 and they swept Kentucky). It was an unbelievable week," he told Kyle Niedderriep of *The Star*. But I found the girls different. I never had an ego-driven episode in my 19 years because of a disenchanted girl.

    One of the things that I did try to do with each 2-week All-Star camp was to offer kids some new experiences. One thing I tried to do every year with the two teams was to take them to the Governor's office to meet the State's top administrator. In my first year rather than going to the Governor's office, Governor Robert Orr invited the team and staff to his home on North Meridian Street for an outdoor picnic and tour of the mansion.

Everyone enjoyed this outing. Subsequent trips included a trip to visit the then Lt. Governor Becky Skillman while Governor Mitch Daniels was in Japan. The players also met Governors Bayh, O'Bannon, and Daniels.

In another year, Governor Daniels invited the players to sit down at his large conference table. Mitch seemed to be pretty well-versed on who some of the players were and where they came from. This "G recognition," of course thrilled the players.

Our visit inevitably and gratefully always ended with a photo of the teams with the Governor. I hope to include at least one—perhaps of our last visits under my direction—of the Governor with the teams, coaches and managers.

Another year we visited and stayed overnight at the School for the Blind with the players staying in the homes given by David Letterman to the SFTB on North College Avenue in Indianapolis. We also visited a small manufacturing plant where many blind or visually impaired employees worked in Indianapolis.

En route to an exhibition game in southern Indiana we paid an instructive 1.5 hour visit to the iconic Indiana Basketball Hall of Fame in New Castle. On at least two or three occasions the group was hosted by the NCAA to hear an informative presentation by a member of the association's compliance office—good information for 18 year-olds about to enroll on scholarships to Division I universities.

As a change of pace we visited a permanent semi-detention facility for Indiana youth who had some kind of altercation with the law. The facility was located on the south side of Greencastle. The All-Stars played games with the young people, had basketball field goal shooting matches with the kids, and then had a group luncheon with our generous hosts. Our All-Stars felt this was one of their best activities during the two-week camp.

We also had well-loved Hoosier basketball heroes at some of our special dinners while in Indianapolis—including two Mr. Basketballs—Hallie Bryant ('53) and Bobby Plump ('54) and others.

I would be remiss if I didn't thank the legions of good-hearted people who made financial and in-kind contributions to the All-Star games over my 19 years as game director.

There were those like the CEO of MCL Cafeterias, Craig McGaughey, who not only provided three bountiful meals each year for my 19 years during the two-week All-Star camp, but has continued to do so since I retired from *The Indianapolis Star* and the games in 2007. Craig has done even more than providing more than 2,500 meals. In 1992 he established the John Wooden MCL All-Star Citizenship Awards to be presented to one All-Star girl and one All-Star boy, based on exemplary scholarship, community volunteer activities, school citizenship, extracurricular activities, and outstanding basketball skills as an Indiana All-Star.

The award included a handsome plaque and a check for $500 for the winners to take back to their school for support of a worthy school project, generally the school library. One year Indiana Bell (now Ameritech) gave each All-Star a check for $250 for their school library at a special downtown luncheon at the Hilton Hotel. A former All-Star and Bell executive was the keynoter at the awards luncheon

Kristin Mattox, Charlestown High School, and Billy Wright, Richmond High School, were chosen the first two winners in 1992.

For 33 years this award has been presented during the All-Star games in Indianapolis. There have been 66 winners, they are:

Regen Seybert, Anderson Highland, Kelcey Mucker, Lawerenceburg, (1993); Tiffany Gooden, Ft. Wayne Snider, and Tige Darner, Anderson Highland, (1994); Lisa Williams, Carmel, Damon Frierson, Ben Davis (1995); Janette Jaqques, Lafayette Jefferson, and Mickey Hosier, Alexandria-Monroe, (1996); Katrina Merriweather, Cathedral, and Michael Menser, Batesville, (1997); Amber Schober, Plainfield, and Patrick Jackson, Delta, (1998)

Also, Kristen Lowry, Logansport, and Jon Holmes, Bloomington South, (1999); Sara Strahm, Ben Davis, and Aaron Thomas, Northridge (2000); Ebba Gebisa, West Lafayette, and Chris Hill, Lawrence North, (2001); Candace Dark, Fountain Central, and Seth Colclasure, Belmont (2002); Amanda Norris,

Shenandoah, and Andrew Hershberger, Goshen (2003); Kristen Lane, Tri Central, and Peter Minchella, Lafayette Harrison, (2004); Dana Beaven, Corydon Central, and Derek Drews, Elkhart, (2005); Ashley Barlow, Pike, Brandon Hopf, Forest Park,(2006); Sha'la Jackson, Ft. Wayne South, and E'Twaun Moore, E. Chicago Central (2007); Brittany Rayburn, Attica, and Tyler Zeller, Washington,(2008); Courtney Osborn, Hamilton Southeastern, and Errick Peck, Cathedral, (2009); Dee Dee Williams, Ben Davis, and Erik Fromm, Bloomington South, (2010); Amanda Corral, Hobart, and Austin Richie, Lowell, (2011),Alex Morton, Penn, and D.J. Balentine, Kokomo (2012).

Many generous friends of Indiana High School basketball have made cash or in-kind investment in *The Indianapolis Star*'s Indiana All-Star basketball games. This has enabled the game's actual managers, the Indiana Basketball Coaches Association, headed by my good friend and former mentor, Steve Witty, to preserve revenue from ticket sales for numerous student scholarships and awards and to reduce the costs of feeding and housing 30-35 players and staff. We were blessed during my time as game director to have volunteer men and women as coaches of the teams, as well as other wonderful individuals who served as sports information directors, working with the media on behalf of the games, a male and a female manager handling all the details of the security of uniforms, basketballs, scorebooks, valuables and to keep it all together. My first boys' team manager was a young man, Joel Rich, a graduate of Twin Lakes High School, who wanted to join the All-Star operation in the worst way when he was in high school. I suggested he get a another year's experience and join the team within a year while he was a freshman at I.U. It was one of the best decisions I have made; fortunately many other fine young men and women followed in his footsteps over the years ahead. Our first female manager was Dee Ann Ramey, now the girls' coach at North Central High School in Indy whose team won a state 4A basketball championship in 2012. Whenever possible I asked willing and interested former All-Stars to fill these duties. I considered it as important as identifying good coaches. Many did.

Significant long term, sustained sponsors have included individuals like Jon Benjamin, Outback Steakhouse partner who for years sponsored our kickoff media luncheon, plus two more meals for the teams each year; Methodist Sports Medicine Group & Orthopedic Specialists provided the teams two trainers and doctors for going on 25 consecutive years. Mike Wynn at National Car Rental provided complimentary first class vehicles for 15 or so years and now Andy Mohr has stepped up to help followed by Cathedral High School. Another serial supporter of the All-Star teams is McDonald's restaurants owned by Randy and Lisa Shields of Indy.

Kokomo and Ben Davis High Schools for many years have provided practice and event sites for the All-Stars as a significant continuing, contribution to the annual event. Kokomo's school administrators have given the go-ahead to use Mr. Stan Mohr's gift bus and its faithful, friendly driver Bob Maxwell for extended All-Star team trips for years. Pat Strong has saved the game director many headaches by scheduling and securing all the game officials for the exhibition games since the Junior All-Star teams were first named by me and the IBCA in 1996.

Singer Jennifer Nicholson of Noblesville always made herself available to render beautifully the national anthem and *Back Home Again in Indiana* for the opening of all games in Indianapolis.

Always of major concern to me was finding an agreeable, invested provider of all the equipment needed to serve two teams and staff. We were extraordinarily well served for years by Adidas and its rep Mike Barnett; by Converse and later by Reebok by Jim DeSalle, by the Indiana Basketball Coaches Association and its generous sponsor New Balance shoes and much more.

For several years Speedline, Inc. gave us excellent uniforms. Other firms that have done likewise in various years have included Phil Morris from Greenfield and Adidas and Mike Barnett. Presently Lids Team Sports provides the teams their personal equipment. So many business firms and thoughtful individuals have donated cash sponsorships and product that it is beyond me to enumerate and recall all of them in the nearly two decades that I was game director of the event. Let me just say that I apologize for not naming every last one of you and extending my sincere appreciation for all you did or have done or are doing to help the All-Star program so that when we put two Indiana teams together each year they will have the best corporate and individual support that is possible to put on the hardwood.

A few other names I want to mention or re-mention for loyal support are Pacers Sports and Entertainment, Ken Keltner, Mark Kinsey and Wilson Sporting Goods, Gatorade, Lids Team Sports, Beazer Homes, Best Choice Fieldhouse, Moeller Printing Company, the University of Indianapolis, Marian University DePauw University, and The Walden Inn (now the Inn at DePauw), which hosted Indiana All-Star teams for a week with very generous rates in a most hospitable environment. DePauw University for a week for almost a decade provided an air-conditioned gymnasium in its Lilly Center and three full courts for nearly 10 years. Steve Santo at the DePauw Food Court sponsored a wonderful banquet each year for the teams. I also want Greencastle businesses to know that all of their support of the All-Star visits to the city over several years for their camp was greatly appreciated—the public autograph sessions at Wal-Mart, the celebration dinners sponsored in part by Almost Home Restaurant and the general support of the Putnam County Convention and Visitors Bureau and the ads they sponsored in the game program each year were immensely appreciated. I know it means a lot to kids who gain Indiana All-Star status. And it should. This all became clear to me as I called the fortunate few, generally during the first couple of weeks of April each year.

This was underscored for me when I was calling the members of the 12-person Girls team in 1982. When I called for our tall-center-to-be, Missy Taylor, of Floyd Central High School, near New Albany, her mother answered because Mrs. Taylor told me her daughter wasn't home.

When I shared the news with her that Missy was selected for the All-Star team, she gushed, "Well, Praise the Lord."

Yes, praise the Lord, because probably another young student-athlete had her prayers answered.

Many All-Star selections were very coy when I called them with the news. Affecting a kind of nonchalance that I assumed was to give me the impression they either expected the call or they didn't want to show too much exuberance.

But the proof was there. When I told a couple of girls they were to be on the team, they expressed their gratitude with controlled emotions on being selected, then apparently placed their hand/s over the phone to muffle any sound and I could hear this: "Mom! Dad, I made the All-Star team!!!" Followed by a muted scream of excitement.

What a pleasure it always was to be able to be the person who fulfilled one of the dreams of a young man or young woman. I think it may have been the best part of being the game director—for many of these kids being an All-Star had been part of their persona for a long, long time, some as far back as grade school I learned.

One of the most memorable calls I made was to an enthusiastic, funny young man from Lafayette, who I found out as I got to know him better, had a *lot* of big dreams. When I informed Richie Hammel, son of the late Jefferson High School coach Jim Hammel, that he had been selected for the team, without pause, he said, "I will put that on my calendar and I think I will be able to accommodate you at that time," he deadpanned. We both laughed and Richie and I over the ensuing months, shared several laughs.

One in particular, I recall. One of our rules was that players would not be in the rooms of the opposite sex. As I was returning to my own room one afternoon, I noticed an open door of a room occupied by two female All-Stars. Inside was Richie, the center of attention, plopped atop a luggage table. "Richie," I said, "Get outta there." He jumped up and quickly disappeared. One of his female audience later told me that when Richie spotted me approaching the room he was visiting, he said, "Oh, Mr. Aikman won't say anything to me!" Wrong, Richie. But Richie had big ideas; the last I heard he was somewhere on the East Coast in school, planning the purchase of a piece of African coastal land for real estate development.

Those kinds of interactions off the court made the All-Star event for me a continuing psycho-drama that I hardly ever failed to enjoy. The players were generally up for a good time, serious when they needed to be, and always anxious to hang another "L" on Kentucky.

When the Indiana Basketball Hall of Fame in late March, 2013, honored its Silver Anniversary team, about 11 or 12 of my first boys' All-Star team from 1988 returned to Indianapolis as honored guests, It was so gratifying to greet several of the men who performed so well in sweeping Kentucky twice 102-82 in Louisville and 112-100 in Market Square Arena. There were lawyers, teachers, coaches, engineers, entrepreneurs and we all shared a hug or high five and well wishes, the residue of being part of one of the great traditions that makes, in my mind, the Indiana-Kentucky All-Star series, one of the most enduring special traditions in this basketball universe we call Hoosier Hysteria.

On April 27 when the Hall of Fame inducts its new female members in Indianapolis, I am sure we'll reprise the joy and camaraderie of the March event all over again when most of the 1988 Girls' All-Star team gathers to be honored on the 25th anniversary of their time on the Indiana All-Star Girls team. I am definitely looking forward to that special evening with another of my teams and a group of friends.

Four

Family Poems

A Yule Rap Song
By Rapper James Patrick Aikman
Dec. 24, 1990
(Christmas Eve with the Extended Aikman Family
at the Country Kitchen in Chrisman, Illinois
and at The Home of the Senior Aikmans)

Well, welcome folks, I really must say
I'm all hopped up about this Christmas Day.

I've done my shoppin' and I've done my fixin'
I've juiced up Donner and I've groomed old Blixen.

Now I've loaded the sleigh and I've been just itchin'
To drop by goodies here at the Kitchen.

Ho Ho … Ho Ho Ho

You all look happy and right well fed
Thanks to my parents for the lavish spread.

We've all gathered 'round from the countryside,
Tho we did a little skiddin' and we did a little slide.

Ho Ho … Ho Ho Ho

You came from Indy and from Saint Louie
Some flights got cancelled and it got a little screwy.
You drove from Arthur and Champaign, too
Dana and Chicago and the Georgia mountains blue

J. Patrick Aikman

Ho Ho … Ho Ho Ho

Christmas Eve in Dana has a ritual all its own
From "the How do You Do" to "It's Time You Head for Home."

Herbie get the Big Box to gather all the trash
Charlotte cuts the cheese to add a little dash.

Ho Ho … Ho Ho Ho

Judy grabs the bows and Shirley snags some, too….
The gifts just fly all over…and the tree gets knocked askew.

Mikie plays the organ….and Kevin plays some more,
We sing some Christmas ditties…then Herbie takes the floor.

Ho Ho … Ho Ho Ho

He thinks we ought to hurry; we're all just to darned slow;
If we're not done by nine, he says, his fuse is gonna' blow;

Now settle down, dear Herbert, just keep it on your chest
says Charlotte, as she smooths his cute red vest.

We notice something missing; it's Charlotte's two new chairs.
Herb, it seems, has stashed them at the top of the nearby stairs.

Ho Ho … Ho Ho Ho

By now the tree is barren……..all gifts unwrapped, I' judge
We pass around the cookies….. look out here comes de fudge.

We try on hats and dresses and coats and neckties blue
Then march into the dining room…to have a bite or two.

On Andy, on Kurtis, on Felicia and Kerry Gayle,
On Patrick and Judy, on Grant and Cindy without fail.

Ho Ho … Ho Ho Ho

Here's Darian and Kevin and Herbert and Shirley
Vince, Charlotte, and Evelyn—It's all just hurley-burley.

To the feast that's set before us—with love and such affection
As we gather 'round the tables … with Herbert's deft direction

It's a wonderful. Christmas together; it's Santa's finest dream
May your stockings all be filled—with Charlotte's thick Bavarian crème.

But now we must conclude … this exciting Christmas rap.
Santa's got to hurry … and take a little nap.

But you hear him exclaim as he vanishes from sight …
Santa loves you, Baby, …and in '91 just hang on tight!

J. Patrick Aikman

A Thanksgiving Day Rap
Executed in Palos Park, Illinois at the Condo Apartments Dining Room of Judy's Parents, Vince and Evelyn Folk November 22, 1990

Well, hello dudes, I'm glad to say
It's nice you're here … for Turkey Day

You all look cool, you all look natty and
It blows my mind … to see my daddy

Gobble, gobble … Gobble, gobble, gobble

Dad does his sight-seein' in Bono-town
Doesn't leave that porch … doesn't get around

Except to the Kitchen to see the folks…
To spread a little cheer … and tell a few jokes

Gobble, gobble … Gobble, gobble, gobble

He's happy with his ewes … and he's happy with his cows
And to make ends meet---he sells his pea fowls

And Charlotte came in her big white Brougham …
Thought she's never get Herb … to leave his home.

She frankly felt she'd never get out …
With a painful heel … and a round of gout.

She's known around Dana for what she can do with spuds
She likes to drive to the Meis store to buy her duds.

She's a darned good neighbor when it comes to the crunch
And I know she coined the phrase … "a little picklely lunch."

Gobble, gobble … Gobble, gobble, gobble

There's another great couple we're here to salute
It's Vincent and Evelyn … and there's no dispute

They're the toast of the Village … they're the toast of the town
But, lordy, folks, do they get around.

Vincent loves to bowl and he shoots a little pool
He's a fix-it man with his handy little tool.

He loves to drive and he loves to travel,
He's never see a map that he couldn't unravel.

When Vince was young … he just got lucky,
Took that Gal right outta Kentucky.

Gobble, gobble … Gobble, gobble, gobble

J. Patrick Aikman

It turned out, folks, he was a mighty good judge,
He married a beauty who was the Queen of Fudge

Fudge, fudge here and fudge, fudge there …
We all lost our sweet tooth in the dentist's chair.

Evelyn likes to cook and she likes to sew
And she shares her wares wherever she goes.

Gobble, gobble … Gobble, gobble, gobble

She likes to read but it's been sorta hard …
'Til she finds that damned little library card.

Enough of this fiddle…enough of this faddle.
This rapper has had it, Gotta hit the saddle.

So goodbye, dudes … we're happy to say …
We loved seein' you … on Turkey Day!

Gobble, gobble … Gobble, gobble, gobble

Ode to Our Friend Paul. B. Kissinger …
To the Good Life
By James Patrick Aikman

There once was a lad from Reading
Where his yo-yo fame was spreading

Ah, he led the Good Life mid laughter and strife
That began, we assume, on the night if his wedding

He learned all the laws of Nature;
He's friendly with its nomenclature.

He always flew high, no horizon could deny
This pilot would be a Mover and Shaker.

He excelled at all manner of things,
He loved what the Good Life brings.

From dining to concerts to sports to travel,
His pathways were smooth; he avoided the gravel

He embraced singing … that made your ears ring,
With barbershop tunes that were fit for a King.

In defense of our culture … he taught overseas
To young military dependents … he put them at ease.

He gave his time freely … on behalf of Ole DePauw,
And enticed these young scholars … to heed Old Gold's call.

He toured every nation; explored every alley,
He now consults with Rand McNally

He went to Tibet … to dilly-dally with the Dahli,
The eclipse was obscured … in a sheer bit of celestial folly

Then there was Indonesia … and Mauritania, too
Germany and Italy … and sunny old Peru.

In all that he did, he imbued it with joy
With Joanne at his side, he became quite a Boy!

On trips for DePauw, he extolled its fame,
Informing alumni … with his upbeat refrain.

DePauw didn't overlook his superb teaching skills,
It rewarded Our Hero with Tucker's 10,000 bills

Ode to Our Friend Paul B. Kissinger At His Retirement Party
By James Patrick Aikman
April 15, 2000
At Almost Home Restaurant

And he went to bat for many a-friend
Rekindling their spirits which may have needed a mend.

We all love "PB" … and Wagsie does, too,
We could describe him as colorful with his very own hue.

And so tonight we salute a dear friend
Let the Good Times roll. Goodnight and Amen!

J. Patrick Aikman

Poem in Celebration of the Wedding of Kerry and Ron
By James Patrick Aikman
Presented at their Reception Oct. 5, 1996
in Atlanta, Georgia

Welcome, friends, to Callanwolde – deep in Dixie, I do declare. To Celebrate the union – of a very special pair.

Let Atlanta burn again – metaphorically, of course, with the brilliance of tonight.
The Yankees have taken Georgia – to observe the troth they plight.

On the one hand there is Ron – computer whiz and gourmet cook.
Jazz entrepreneur and golfer – who learned by Kellogg's book.

Oh, he's affable and charming – with an impish grin to boot. Kerry even goes so far – to insist he's rather cute.

His interests are far-ranging – from architecture to the cats. He has spontaneity – to which we'll tip our hats.

Yes, Ron, we think you're special – thoughtful, kind and caring, too.
We're delighted you're now family – our blessings we imbue.

(continued on next page)

141

As for the bride, our Kerry, that subject we now address.
She develops strategies – to lower clients' stress.

Her soothing, probing questions – have always been her style.
To fathom others' feelings – and to eliminate the guile.

It all began at Butler – in the Kappa house, we guess.
Where she learned to analyze – the Sisters of the crest.

Then on to No Hope Hospital – and psychiatric chores –
To minister to the needy – and supervise the wards and floors.

"Is it summer?" Judy 'd say. "Time for another move?"
We'd gather up the tarp, ropes and maps – and
get back in the transport groove.

Xavier and Cincinnati – key stops along the way.
Thence Charleston and Evanston – she
literally kept truckin' every day.

She landed at Loyola to start the doctoral grind.
And persevered to earn it – with honors, we would find.

J. Patrick Aikman

But she came across something else – in a
near Northside neighborhood.
On a blind date to Weed's – she turned up something extra good.

A relationship so natural – that it matured as months went by.
And grew to love and admiration – between this gal and guy.

They enhanced the life of their partner
– opening vistas new to each.
Sought and found their own persona – but working
together – made their grasp exceed their reach.

And so today we gather – to affirm the love they share –
May their lives together be enhanced – and
for each other may they always care.

Let us now raise a toast to our newlywed
couple – here's to Ron and Kerry.

A Visit to Grandpa's Jot 'Em Down Store in Logan, Illinois*

By Gertrude James Aikman

The nicest place for little boys
Is out in Logan, Illinois
At Grandpa's store, the Jot 'Em Down,
The very finest store in town.

If you like candy bars and cokes'
Or chewing gum or funny jokes
Just come to Grandpa's Jot 'Em Down
And stand in line with all the town.

When we start out for Illinois,
My Dad will say, "Remember, boys,
Don't pick up things because they're handy
Or hint around for cakes and candy."

If Mike says, "Daddy, don't you think
We might ask Grandpa for a drink?"
Then Mother says, (she's Grandpa's daughter)
"Be sure to say, "A drink of water."

(continued on next page)

J. Patrick Aikman

But Grandpa's not like other folks.
When we say "water," he brings Cokes
And everything that's fine and dandy
Like crackerjack and peanut candy.

And all the time, he's cracking jokes
And asking us about our folks
And when it comes to ice-cream cones
There's no one like my Grandpa Jones.

And so, remember, girls and boys,
To go to Logan, Illinois
And drive around about the town
'Til you find Grandpa's Jot 'Em Down.

Just drop in any day or night,
My Grandpas Jones will treat you right.
Thank you a lot and if you like
Say you were sent by Pat and Mike.

*A poem written by my Grandmother Aikman of Dana prior to a visit to My Grandpa Jones' Rural Store in Logan, Illinois

A Belated Birthday Poem for Michael Aikman
By Grandpa Pat Aikman
Dec. 29, 2011

I am going to write a poem
About my grandson Mike
He's been a high achiever
Ever since he was a tyke

He's awesome in all sports
Maybe baseball is his best
He tires so hard to help his team
And he passes every test

In basketball he does well, too
At the power forward post
And if I'm not real careful
You'll surely think I boast.

And what if I do—
Rant and rave and emit a loud, long cheer;
Do you think it will really hurt us
If I say "Atta, boy." Way to go grandson, Michael Kurtis!

(continued on next page)

J. Patrick Aikman

He's studious, that's for sure.
He usually makes straight A's
Add with his acting and guitar play,
He readily earns one's praise.

He loves his teacher, Sarah Awe,
His friends are dear to him
Andrew-Will-Tim, Sam and Luke
Will enliven any gym.

When they went to b-camp at Taylor
We notified local cops,
That if you messed with this comedic squad
You'd get one—in the chops

An Original Poem for Emma Nicole Aikman on Her 13th Birthday
By Grandpa Pat Aikman
Oct. 4, 2011

I've tried and tried and looked so hard
To find you a ... swell birthday card

There's nothing there—upon the shelves
That would even interest, little elves

And now I think, upon this day,
When you were born and came our way

How lucky we were you came to stay
You chose the guitar and how to play

As you are maturing and will do your thing.
Making music and wearing bling.

We are so proud of all you've done
All the games you play ... and the medals you've won

(continued on next page)

J. Patrick Aikman

All the "A's" on your report
It seems you never come up short

And better yet, you do your part
To make life beautiful through your art

So much talent … such a sweet, nice gal.
I'm sure you'll soon be some guy's pal.

So, Emma, dear, we are so proud
Of all you've done; you exceed the crowd

At 13 years you've done so much
Now hit that pedal and engage the clutch

You're on the road to much, much more
There's hardly time to keep your score

But a moment now, we must take
To douse the candles and cut the cake

We rejoice with you, our precious dear
To more successes throughout your year.

Poem Written for my Grandchildren Emma and Michael Aikman

as they Prepared to Go on Spring Break with their Dad to Utah and Nevada to Visit a Friend of their Father
By Grandpa Pat Aikman

Spring vacations are for fun
In the Canyon and in the sun
Buy a Coke or candy bar
Travel near and travel far
Please be safe if you use skis
Avoid avalanches, if you please!
Wish that I could be with you …
But I have other things to do.
Like keeping Asbury folks in line
And finding time to sleep and dine.
Enjoy your time with your pappy
You're young just once…so smile, be happy!

J. Patrick Aikman

Another Vacation Send-off Poem for my Grandchildren Emma and Michael Aikman
By Grandpa Pat Aikman
March 25, 2012

I heard you're off on a fine, grand trip
Enjoy yourself and take a dip
In any pool that's near at hand
And splash a bit in a way so grand.
You'll look back as years go by
And recall this trip and maybe sigh
We went with Dad way out west
We had a trip that was the Best
We shared good times and laughed a lot
But in Las Vegas we never won a pot
These good memories will last a long, long time
So don't forget this little rhyme.
Enjoy yourself on this spring break
And plenty of shut-eye you'll want to take.

Foreign Aid for a Comrade's Improved Office On the Ground Floor

A monetary gift to my son-in-law (who coaches kids for SAT and ACT tests) to decorate and renew his new office space in their home's basement. (Ron's wife is a doctor who treats patients with eating (tummy) disorders)
By James Patrick Aikman
May 8, 2012

You've got the essence of an office … in the room that's down below.
I recollect you called it the 'dungeon" … if your really want to know.

I've thought about the problem facing Ron and Kerry
About where you'll pursue your days' work that's really not too hairy.

I took an inventory of contents … of the room that's down below
And concluded … that some of it … really ought to go.

Keep the guitar and keyboard to sustain you,
though musically you are not,
Toss the Neil Young poster and the globe, … instead, think of Camelot.

Chuck the fancy throw rug … dismiss the blue dish on the window sill,
And conjure up a corner office suite … that's guaranteed to thrill.

Ah, the neo-dungeon has its attributes … it's quiet … And remote
Where you can curse the computer's foibles…
and pray you coach no dolts

Yes, Ron has made a sacrifice … to compromise on this score,
And gentlemanly yielded to higher authority
… on the upper floor …

Where Kerry works on her magic for the tummies of the town,
Determined not to let her busy schedule …ever get her down.

Unwisely, poppa may be wading … Into this domestic battle
With this poetry …and attempt …at meaningless, useless prattle.

So if I may make an offer …of a few ($200) Hoosier bucks
So that you'll never have to say or feel …
Oh, … this damned place sucks!"

DISCLAIMER

Any resemblance between the message in this poem and the actual truth of the domestic situation in the household known as Michalak-Aikman is simply due to perhaps inappropriate, inordinate poetic license on the part of the foreign author of this presentation and is in no way meant to judge or evaluate the efficacy of whether a second office at 4420 S. Grimes Ave. in Edina, Minnesota, should now or ever be situated, developed or decorated to house the ever-expanding Breakaway Test Prep enterprise successfully launched and nurtured by the Honorable Ron Michalak, SAT, ACT, ESQ.

In other words, this is written all in fun, folks!